31 MEN OF THE BIBLE

WHO THEY WERE AND WHAT WE CAN LEARN FROM THEM TODAY

TABLE OF CONTENTS

INTRODUCTION

At first glance, it seems the men featured in this book share little common ground. From a socioeconomic perspective, their positions couldn't have been more diverse. Job enjoyed wealth and privilege for a time, lost everything, but then gained it all back. King Solomon may very well have been the wealthiest man who ever lived. John the Baptist opted for a hermit's existence in the wilderness, feeding on locusts and wild honey. The apostle Peter worked a blue-collar job as a fisherman.

Their stories in the Bible follow a multitude of trajectories.

- The account of Moses stretches across four Old Testament books, spanning the 120 years of his life.

- The four Gospels cover Jesus' birth extensively, go silent for almost 30 years, and then pick up the story during the last three years of his life.

- The accounts of Jonah, Nathan, Shadrach, Meshach, and Abednego involve little more than single incidents in each man's life.

- Zacchaeus's appearance lasts for all of 10 verses—the duration of one brief conversation with Jesus.

Their character and personalities certainly don't fit neatly into a single category either.

Joseph, Elijah, and Daniel were role models for the ages, exemplifying courage, faithfulness, and grace under fire. Jacob, Samson, and David were flawed heroes at best, men who were used by God in powerful ways despite their poor choices and personal failures. King Saul and Judas Iscariot were consumed by their dark desires and are remembered primarily as villains.

In fact, the only common ground of significance these men share is that their stories appear in the pages of God's Word. God deemed their experiences—good and bad—as worthy of inclusion in his book.

And that's reason enough to warrant further study.

After all, God reveals himself in Scripture not only through the commandments he issues but also in the ways he interacts with people. We can draw conclusions about his mercy and forgiveness from the way he restores his relationship with David after the king's despicable treatment of Uriah. We can take comfort in his protection and plan because he proves to Joseph that no circumstances are beyond his power to change.

By the same token, we get a sense of his holiness and wrath from the way he punishes Adam's disobedience. We get glimpses of his awesome power in his dealings with Jonah, as the prophet tries to resist his plan.

If we're wise, we'll use the stories of these men as inspiration or cautionary tales in our own relationships with God. We'll work to emulate the kind of sacrificial obedience Shadrach, Meshach, and Abednego demonstrated; the kind of humility and courage Gideon showed; or the kind of bold evangelism Peter and Paul practiced.

Toward that end, our desire is that you draw from these men's stories wisdom, inspiration, and application for your own life.

In the pages that follow, you'll find a concise summary of each man's appearance in Scripture, viewed through the lens of our modern culture; surprising revelations that may cause you to rethink what you thought you knew about each man; Bible passages that capture the essence of each man's experience; helpful prompts for applying the principles of each man's story to your own life; and thought-provoking questions to help you find common ground with these heroes of the Christian faith.

As you work your way through this volume, you'll find that the bedrock principles of God's Word are as applicable today as they were thousands of years ago. You'll discover that the stories of these men are living history. The timeless truths that guided these heroes of the faith will guide you as well.

5

May God richly bless you as you read *31 Men of the Bible*.

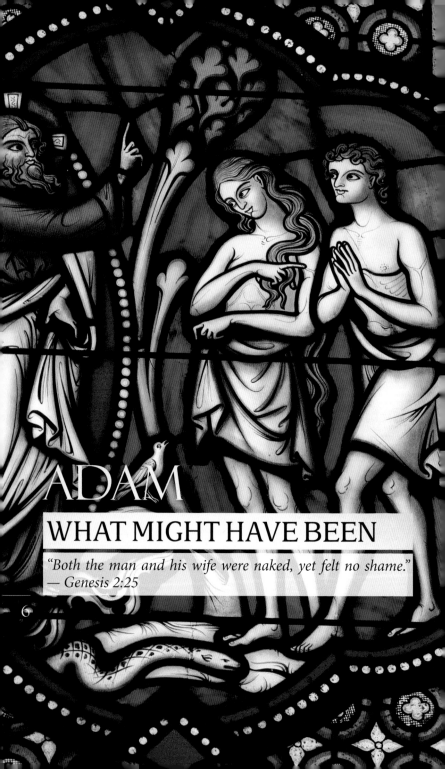

ADAM

WHAT MIGHT HAVE BEEN

"Both the man and his wife were naked, yet felt no shame."
— Genesis 2:25

f all the men in the Bible, only two knew what it was like to have a personal, untainted, unobstructed relationship with God himself. One was Jesus, the Son of God. The other was Adam.

Adam experienced life in Eden—a name that's become synonymous with *paradise*, and for good reason. Eden was God's showcase. On display in this garden paradise was nature in perfect harmony, as the Creator intended. Genesis 2:9 says God filled the garden with trees that were "pleasing in appearance and good for food." Imagine the beauty, the wonder, the divine artistry that Adam enjoyed.

God gave Adam the responsibility of working the garden and caring for it. But this was not a burdensome task. Based on how the nature of work changed later as part of the curse (see Gen 3:17–19), we may assume that Adam derived deep satisfaction and a sense of fulfillment from his work in the garden. It's very likely that his God-given responsibilities meshed perfectly with his gifts and abilities.

God told Adam to "rule the fish of the sea, the birds of the sky, and every creature that crawls on the earth" (Gen 1:28). He brought every animal and bird to Adam to be named. Whatever Adam called each creature became its name.

Only Adam could explain what it was like to live on earth with only God himself and the animals as companions. Only Adam could describe the experience of waking from a deep slumber to find his female counterpart—his perfect companion and complement—next to him.

Adam walked with God—not in a metaphorical sense, but in a two-friends-taking-leisurely-evening-strolls-together way (see Gen 3:8). Adam enjoyed God's company, and God enjoyed his.

Adam experienced a clean conscience. He knew what it was like to be naked and unashamed. Such was life in Eden.

Ultimately, though, Eden was not enough for Adam. The one rule God put in place—"You must not eat from the tree of the knowledge of good and evil" (Gen 2:17)—proved to be too restricting for Adam. He let temptation get the better of him. Along with his wife, Eve, he disobeyed God and ate of the fruit.

And everything changed in an instant.

Genesis 3 describes the consequences of their actions. "The eyes of both of them were opened, and they knew they were naked" (v. 7). They experienced guilt and shame for the first time.

Then when God came to walk in the garden at the time of the evening breeze, Adam didn't join him. Instead, he hid from his Creator, his Sustainer, his Friend. Never again in his lifetime would Adam be able to interact with his heavenly Father unashamedly.

The punishment for Adam and Eve's sin altered the human experience. Among other things, the work that had once brought pleasure and fulfillment would become difficult and painful. And with the ideal of Eden corrupted, Adam and Eve were evicted from the garden. For the rest of their lives, they were forced to make their way in an inhospitable world.

More devastating than all of that, though, was the transformation Adam experienced in his relationship with God. Guilt and shame eroded the innocence that had once marked Adam's life. Bitterness and hard-heartedness followed until the ideals of Eden were nothing but a memory. Intimacy was lost.

In addition to guilt and shame, Adam wrestled with unimaginable regret for the rest of his life. Genesis 5:5 says that "Adam's life lasted 930 years." For over nine centuries, then, he was left to wonder what might have been.

The good news is that God took the steps that humankind could not take to restore the relationship ruined by Adam's disobedience. In his unfathomable grace, God sent his Son to pay the penalty for Adam's sin—and for the sins of every one of Adam's descendants. Jesus' death and resurrection make it possible for believers to stand before God uncorrupted, as Adam did, and to have a personal, intimate relationship with him.

THE TAKEAWAY

A popular aphorism asks, "If you feel distant from God, guess who moved?" It serves as a reminder that sin and disobedience don't get the final word in our relationship with God—not as long as his grace is available to us. First John 1:9 says, "If we confess our sins, He is faithful and righteous to forgive us our sins and to cleanse us from all unrighteousness."

We don't have to endure the desolation and separation Adam experienced. For every barrier we put up in our relationship with God, whether it be a sinful habit or a decision that doesn't honor him, he offers a chance to remove it.

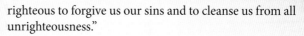

FOOD FOR THOUGHT

1. What specific choices, habits, or attitudes have disrupted your relationship with God?

2. What does the promise of 1 John 1:9 mean to you?

3. What advice would you give to someone who feels like Adam—completely separated from God because of sinful choices?

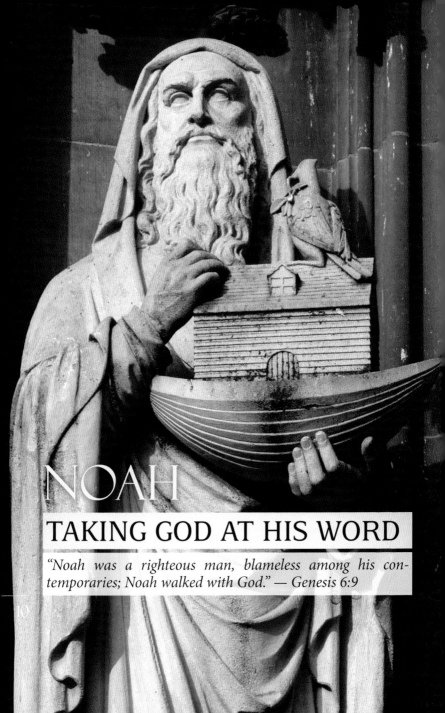

NOAH

TAKING GOD AT HIS WORD

"Noah was a righteous man, blameless among his contemporaries; Noah walked with God." — Genesis 6:9

he story of Noah's ark is so familiar that the details, especially those concerning Noah himself, tend to get overlooked. As is the case with other heroes of the faith, the Bible doesn't say why Noah "found favor in the sight of the LORD" (Gen 6:8).

But clues do exist. Consider the instructions God laid out over the course of nine verses in Genesis 6. In one massive piece of exposition, God revealed to Noah his plan to destroy the earth and those on it. The only land-dwelling beings who would survive his judgment were those Noah would house in a floating sanctuary.

God instructed Noah to

- build an ark of gopher wood that was 450 long, 75 feet wide, and 45 feet high;

- install three decks, a door, various rooms, and a roof, according to specifications;

- cover the entire vessel with pitch—inside and out;

- lead two of every animal (male and female) into the ark and group them accordingly inside;

- gather and secure every kind of food that is eaten for the journey; and

- enter the ark with his family.

How does a person respond to such an overwhelming assignment? According to Genesis 6:22, Noah "did everything that God had commanded him."

What a remarkable reaction. The directions from God were unprecedented, to say the least. No one had ever been instructed to do anything like that previously. There were no templates to follow, no previous ark-building experiences to draw from, no end-of-the-world-disaster-preparedness manuals to consult.

Yet Noah did *everything* God commanded him. He didn't panic. He didn't use his inexperience as an excuse. He didn't call for backup. He didn't even ask, "Why me?"

Could it be that Noah had an inkling of why God had given him such an assignment? Is it possible that he realized he had certain skills that he could apply to the task?

His response implies confidence—in himself, to a small degree perhaps, but in God to a much larger degree. Noah seems to have recognized that

God would not entrust such an assignment to someone who was incapable of fulfilling it.

Whatever self-doubt he might have faced was overmatched by his God-certainty. So Noah used the personal tools available to him, whether small-scale carpentry skills, a knack for organization and design, a familiarity with available resources, or a dedicated line of communication with God. And he trusted God to do something incredible with the results.

Likewise, during his time on the ark, Noah must have drawn on reserves of patience, ingenuity, and resourcefulness that he didn't know he possessed just to keep his family sane and focused. They had, after all, just experienced the end of the world as they knew it. Their future was uncertain. And the conditions on the ark probably did little to improve their emotional well-being. Yet Noah, using the tools of persuasion and encouragement at his disposal, helped them focus on their roles in God's plan.

In addition to his family responsibilities, Noah was to care for the animals. It's reasonable to assume that his zoological expertise up to that point was limited to the care and feeding of livestock. Suddenly he found himself the caretaker of countless species facing extinction. His job was to keep them fed, watered, and protected, in close quarters, for as long as it took the floodwaters to recede.

Though details of life in the ark are scarce in Scripture, we may conclude that Noah used the skills he had to the best of his ability and relied on God to make the most of them.

And that's exactly what God did. He kept his protective hand over Noah and his family. He equipped Noah with everything he needed to fulfill his responsibilities. He blessed Noah's efforts and multiplied them according to his plan. He rewarded Noah's faithfulness.

So when Noah and his precious cargo disembarked from their vessel—after spending more than a year on board—they had everything they needed to replenish the earth.

Ever the faithful servant, Noah built an altar and offered sacrifices to the Lord as soon as his feet touched the ground. For all his heroic accomplishments in building the ark, rounding up the animals, and navigating the most catastrophic event in human history, Noah knew exactly who deserved the praise and glory.

This probably explains why God chose to use him for such an extraordinary task.

THE TAKEAWAY

God equips people with certain skills and abilities—some are obvious; others aren't. You may not realize you possess certain gifts until circumstances call for them.

God also places people in certain situations at certain times for very specific reasons. If you maintain a spirit of bold obedience and faithfulness in those situations, you can make a lasting impact in the lives of other people and in your own life as well.

FOOD FOR THOUGHT

1. With what skills, abilities, and spiritual gifts has God blessed you?

2. Give some examples of how you've been able to put those gifts to use in the past.

3. How might God multiply your gifts and abilities to accomplish something far beyond what you think is possible?

13

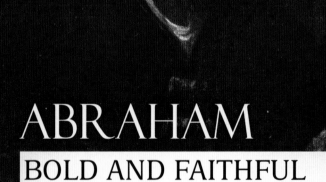

ABRAHAM

BOLD AND FAITHFUL

"[Abraham] believed the LORD, and He credited it to him as righteousness." — Genesis 15:6

he Bible doesn't say why God selected Abraham to serve as the progenitor of his people, the "father of all who believe" (Rom 4:11). But it's likely that the man's willingness to obey, regardless of circumstances, played a role in the Lord's decision. Abraham's bold faithfulness and fearless approach to serving God certainly set him apart from his contemporaries.

When God told Abraham to take his wife, Sarah, and his nephew Lot and leave his homeland and everything he had known for the first 75 years of his life to go to some distant land called Canaan, Abraham pulled up stakes and ventured into the unknown.

When the time came for Abraham and his nephew Lot to go their separate ways, Abraham gave his nephew first choice as to where he would settle. Lot chose the well-watered Jordan Valley near the city of Sodom. Abraham took what was left, confident that God would help him prosper, regardless of Lot's selection.

When God revealed his intention to destroy the cities of Sodom and Gomorrah because of the wickedness of their inhabitants, Abraham, in a stunning display of compassion and courage, humbly urged God to consider the people who weren't wicked. "What if there are 50 righteous people in the city? Will You really sweep it away instead of sparing the place for the sake of the 50 righteous people who are in it? . . . Suppose the 50 righteous lack five. Will you destroy the whole city for lack of five?" (Gen 18:24, 28).

Abraham negotiated the number down to 40, then 30, and then 20. Mustering his last bit of courage, Abraham convinced God to spare the city if just 10 righteous people could be found there (see Gen 18:22–33). Alas, it turned out that not even 10 righteous people could be found in Sodom and Gomorrah, so both cities were destroyed when God caused burning sulfur to rain down on them (see Gen 19:23–25).

Abraham's relationship with God wasn't all peaks, of course. His renowned boldness and courage occasionally deserted him. On his way to Canaan, for instance, Abraham had to pass through Gerar. Abraham feared that the king of that land would take an interest in Sarah, who was very beautiful, and have him killed. So he told Sarah to tell the king that she was his sister, and not his wife. Abraham allowed Sarah to be taken away and allowed the king to give him flocks, herds, slaves, and camels for the privilege of marrying his "sister." Ultimately, though, the truth came out, and Abraham and Sarah were sent on their way.

And when God promised Abraham and Sarah that they would have a son, even though they were very old, they underestimated his power to make it happen naturally. Sarah gave Abraham her much younger handmaiden, Hagar. With Hagar, Abraham produced a son and named him Ishmael.

But that was not God's plan at all. When Sarah eventually gave birth to Isaac, conflict developed between Abraham's two "families." The tension became so unbearable that Abraham was forced to send Hagar and Ishmael away, into the wilderness, where they would have to make their way on their own (with God's help).

When Abraham had an opportunity to redeem himself, however, he showed what bold faithfulness *really* looks like. God presented Abraham one day with perhaps the most gut-wrenching command in all of Scripture. He instructed Abraham to offer a burnt sacrifice to him—only, instead of killing a lamb for the sacrifice, Abraham was to kill his beloved son Isaac.

Abraham didn't negotiate this time. He didn't question God or hesitate. He immediately made the necessary preparations, gathered Isaac, and set out for the place where the sacrifice was to be made. When they arrived, he prepared the altar and laid Isaac on top of it.

Genesis 22:10–12 picks up the story from there:

> Then Abraham reached out and took the knife to slaughter his son.
>
> But the Angel of the Lord called to him from heaven and said, "Abraham, Abraham!"
>
> He replied, "Here I am."
>
> Then He said, "Do not lay a hand on the boy or do anything to him. For now I know that you fear God, since you have not withheld your only son from Me."

Abraham demonstrated the depths of his bold faithfulness under the most extreme circumstances imaginable. And he learned how generously God rewards such faithfulness when God said,

> "I will indeed bless you and make your offspring as numerous as the stars of the sky and the sand on the seashore. Your offspring will possess the gates of their enemies. And all the nations of the earth will be blessed by your offspring because you have obeyed My command." (Gen 22:17–18)

THE TAKEAWAY

If you know the right thing to do in a given situation, do it boldly. Don't be cowed by criticism, second-guessing, or self-doubt. God blesses those who are faithful to his will.

FOOD FOR THOUGHT

1. On a scale of 1 to 10, how bold are you in your Christian faith? (For the sake of comparison, let's say Abraham was a 9.) Give some examples to support your answer.

2. What specific obstacles keep you from being bolder?

3. In what ways does God reward bold faithfulness today?

JACOB

THE QUEST FOR RECONCILIATION

"'Your name will no longer be Jacob,' He said. 'It will be Israel because you have struggled with God and with men and have prevailed.'" — Genesis 32:28

acob entered the world grasping—literally. The second twin boys, Jacob started his life journey by grasping h... Esau's heel. The symbolism is difficult to ignore. Jacob wanted what was his—and then some.

What he wanted most was Esau's birthright. In the culture of the Old Testament, being the firstborn son was everything. The firstborn received a double portion of inheritance and a special blessing from his father.

Jacob saw his opportunity to secure these for himself one day when his brother, Esau, came back from a hunt. Esau was famished, and Jacob just happened to be cooking lentil stew. Jacob offered his brother some in exchange for his birthright. That Esau agreed to the exchange shows how little he cared for the birthright, but that doesn't absolve Jacob of his deceitfulness.

Securing the birthright itself was only half the equation, though. In order for Jacob to get everything he wanted, he needed his father's blessing, which was irrevocable. Working for him was the fact that his father, Isaac, was old and nearly blind. Going against him was the fact that his appearance was nothing like his brother's. For one thing, Esau was hairy; Jacob was smooth-skinned.

That's where Rebekah, Jacob's mother, stepped in to help. While Esau was out hunting, Rebekah disguised Jacob by putting animal furs on his arms and neck. The ruse worked. Jacob tricked Isaac into giving him the blessing of the firstborn. His usurping of Esau was complete.

Esau was furious when he learned what his brother had done. He vowed to kill Jacob after their father's death. Rebekah learned of his plan, however, and sent Jacob to live with Laban, a relative in a distant land. There he would be safe.

While living with Laban, Jacob fell in love with Laban's younger daughter, Rachel. Laban offered to give Jacob his daughter's hand in marriage in exchange for seven years of labor. But the morning after Jacob's wedding, he discovered that Laban had substituted his older daughter, Leah, for Rachel.

In order to marry Rachel, too, Jacob agreed to work seven *more* years for Laban. It seems that those who live by deception find themselves deceived.

In the years that followed, Jacob's wives (and their handmaidens) bore him 12 sons—who would be the basis for the 12 tribes of Israel.

Jacob himself amassed a tremendous amount of wealth. He seemed to have everything a man could want—except closure.

As time went by, Jacob felt a great need to reconcile with his brother. As far as Jacob knew, Esau still wanted him dead. Yet he was willing to risk everything he had, including his life, for the chance to make things right. He packed up everything he owned and journeyed with his family back to his homeland. He sent gifts of oxen, donkeys, flocks, and slaves ahead of him, hoping to appease Esau. Jacob soon received a message: Esau was riding out to meet him—with 400 men in tow.

Before he met with Esau, however, Jacob had to contend with one other person. According to Genesis 32, Jacob wrestled all night with a mysterious man. When the man saw he couldn't defeat Jacob, he struck Jacob, dislocating his hip. Still Jacob refused to let go of the man until he blessed him. "'Your name will no longer be Jacob,' He said. 'It will be Israel because you have struggled with God and with men and have prevailed'" (v. 28).

That struggle had just been resolved when Esau and his men approached Jacob. Gathering his courage, Jacob walked out to meet Esau and his men alone. He bowed to the ground seven times as he approached, humbling himself before the brother he had wronged so many years earlier.

Jacob's fears were quelled when he saw Esau running to meet him. The two men hugged, kissed, and wept together. Esau refused Jacob's gifts on the grounds that he, too, was a wealthy man. But Jacob insisted. He had a debt to repay.

The Bible says little about their post-reunion interaction. We're left with a picture of reconciliation. The relationship that had once been a source of contention for the brothers became a source of comfort and connection.

THE TAKEAWAY

Jacob spent most of his life running from his family—specifically, his brother. Yet when he finally faced his problem, he found forgiveness and restoration.

Jacob's experience reveals three keys to genuine reconciliation. The first is a spirit of confession and humility. You have to admit your own wrongdoing.

The second is courage. You must boldly make the first move to bridge the distance between you. You have to make yourself vulnerable and risk rejection.

The third is the involvement of the Almighty. Ask God to give you the wisdom to interact with the person in a way that promotes reconciliation.

FOOD FOR THOUGHT

1. Think of a relationship in your life that is estranged. What role have you played in the estrangement?

2. What specific step could you take to help restore the relationship?

3. For what would you most need God's help in order to take that step?

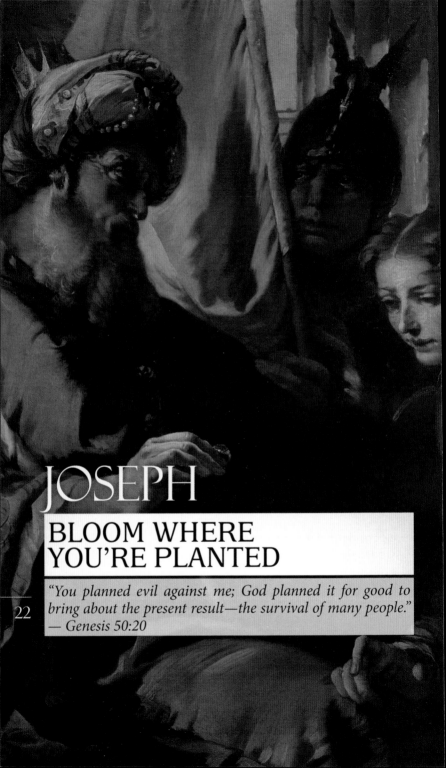

JOSEPH

BLOOM WHERE YOU'RE PLANTED

"You planned evil against me; God planned it for good to bring about the present result—the survival of many people." — Genesis 50:20

oseph had an extraordinary ability to shine in the darkest of places, to thrive under circumstances that could have crushed his spirit. He demonstrated this ability early.

Joseph's 10 older brothers hated him because their father, Jacob, loved him—much more than he loved the rest of his children. He lavished attention and gifts on Joseph while the rest of his sons burned with envy.

Joseph refused to be intimidated by his brothers' hatred and bullying. He boldly recounted his prophetic, God-given dreams in which his entire family bowed down to him. Of course, that made his brothers even angrier.

So one day they got rid of him. They sold Joseph to slave traders who were traveling to Egypt and then made their father think he'd been killed by a wild animal. In Egypt, the slave traders sold Joseph to a government official named Potiphar. And Joseph was faced with the prospect of being a lowly servant in a foreign land for the rest of his life.

Joseph didn't curl up into a ball of self-pity. Instead, he worked hard to become the best servant in Potiphar's household. And Potiphar took notice. He recognized Joseph's skills and potential—not to mention the way Joseph's God seemed to bless everything he did—and put Joseph in charge of his entire household.

That's when Potiphar's wife started taking a romantic interest in Joseph. Unfortunately, when Joseph rebuffed her advances, she accused him of attempted rape. Joseph was thrown into prison.

Joseph truly understood what it feels like to hit rock bottom. He had no one to help him, no hope for release. So what did he do? He worked hard to become a model prisoner. And before long, the warden put him in charge of everything that went on inside the prison.

When Pharaoh's cupbearer and baker were thrown into prison, Joseph befriended them. And when they both had dreams filled with meaningful symbolism, Joseph interpreted the dreams using his God-given skills. The cupbearer received good news: according to Joseph, his dream meant that in three days Pharaoh would restore him to his old position. The baker was not so fortunate: his dream meant that in three days he would be executed.

Three days later Joseph's predictions came true. When the cupbearer was released from prison, Joseph asked him to put in a good word with Pharaoh. But the cupbearer forgot all about Joseph for two years—until Pharaoh himself had a couple of disturbing dreams.

In the first, the king was standing by the Nile River when seven healthy cows emerged and started grazing among the reeds. They were followed by seven sickly cows, who promptly devoured the healthy ones. In the second dream, Pharaoh saw seven healthy heads of grain growing on a single stalk. They were followed by seven scorched heads, which swallowed up the healthy ones.

When no one else could interpret the dreams, the cupbearer remembered and suggested Joseph. Pharaoh sent for him immediately. Imagine the pressure of going straight from prison to the palace, with the eyes of the king's entire court on you. Many people would have wilted under such scrutiny, but not Joseph. Joseph trusted his God-given skills.

With confidence he told Pharaoh that the seven healthy cows and seven healthy heads of grain represented seven years of abundance for Egypt. The seven emaciated cows and seven scorched heads of grain represented seven years of famine that would follow.

Furthermore, he advised Pharaoh to appoint a wise leader to oversee preparations for the famine. This leader would need to make sure that one-fifth of the grain collected during the years of abundance was put into long-term storage. Pharaoh gave the job to Joseph, making him second-in-command over all of Egypt.

When the famine hit, people from across the region came to Egypt to buy food. Among them were Joseph's brothers. They didn't recognize Joseph as their sibling, but they did recognize him as the Egyptian official who could save their lives. So they bowed down to him.

Joseph could have exacted a dark revenge on his brothers for what they'd done to him so many years earlier. Instead, he chose to see God's hand in his circumstances. He recognized that he was in a position to save his family—not to mention Egypt and the surrounding nations—from the famine precisely because of what *God* had done in his life.

THE TAKEAWAY

Attitude often dictates success. Joseph had no reason for hope in Egypt. Yet he didn't give in to despair, anger, or self-pity. He took everything that was thrown at him and built something substantial with it.

He made the best of his situation. And when his situation changed, he made the best of that as well. He never lost sight of who he was or what he had to offer. He found opportunities to shine in the darkest of circumstances. As a result, he was used mightily by the Lord.

FOOD FOR THOUGHT

1. How did you react the last time you faced a difficult circumstance?

2. What did you learn from the experience? What do you hope to do differently next time?

3. On what God-given skills and abilities can you lean when circumstances grow dark?

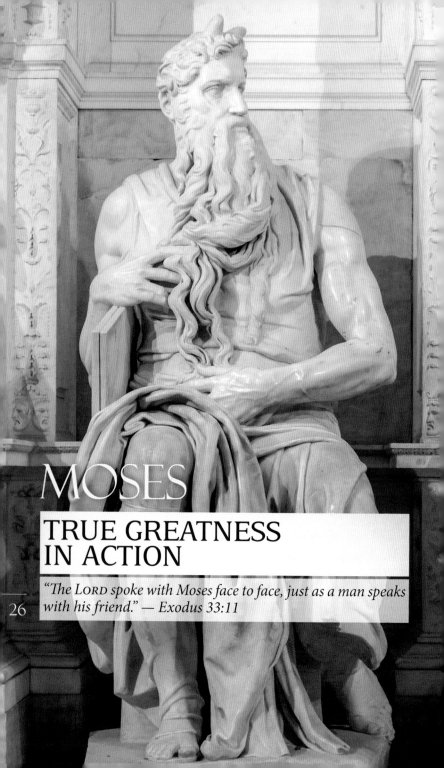

MOSES

TRUE GREATNESS
IN ACTION

"The LORD *spoke with Moses face to face, just as a man speaks with his friend." — Exodus 33:11*

hakespeare said, "Some men are born great, some men achieve greatness, and some have greatness thrust upon them." All three statements seem to apply to Moses.

The circumstances of his birth certainly suggest a life of greatness. Moses was born a Hebrew slave in Egypt at a time when all Hebrew babies in the land were being executed. To save his life, his mother placed him in a watertight basket and floated him down the Nile. There he was discovered—and adopted—by the daughter of Pharaoh, king of Egypt (see Exod 2:1–10).

In Pharaoh's household, Moses was trained to be a great leader of men. His future seemed limitless—until the day he saw an Egyptian overseer beating a Hebrew slave. Stepping in to protect the slave—one of his own people—Moses killed the Egyptian. This incurred the wrath of Pharaoh, who sought revenge on Moses (see Exod 2:11–15).

Moses thus became a fugitive. He escaped to the wilderness, where he built a new life for himself by tending flocks. His life on the run was interrupted by an encounter with God, who appeared to him in the midst of a burning bush and, in essence, "thrust greatness" upon Moses (see Exodus 3).

The highlights of Moses' story are familiar to anyone who's seen the movie *The Ten Commandments*. Moses returned to Egypt to confront Pharaoh and demand the release of all Hebrew slaves. When Pharaoh refused, Moses (along with his brother, Aaron) called down plagues on Egypt, including all the water in Egypt turning to blood; swarms of frogs, gnats, flies, and locusts; the death of livestock; boils; hail; total darkness; and the death of every firstborn son (see Exod 7:14–11:10).

Pharaoh relented and allowed Moses to lead the Hebrews out of Egypt. He quickly changed his mind, though, and chased them down with his army, trapping them on the shores of the Red Sea. With the Egyptian forces bearing down on them, Moses lifted his hands as God instructed, and the waters of the Red Sea parted, allowing the Hebrews to walk across on dry land. When the Egyptians tried to follow, the waters came together, killing them all.

Moses led the Hebrews through the wilderness to the promised land. Along the way, God provided them with manna and quail to eat. He sent water flowing from rocks to quench their thirst. Yet still the people complained and longed for their old lives as slaves in Egypt.

When they arrived at Sinai, the people camped at the base of the mountain while Moses ascended it to meet with God and receive his commandments on two stone tablets. When Moses came back down, he found the Hebrews worshipping a golden calf they had made (see Exod 32:1–29). Such was life for the leader of these stubborn, infuriating, easily tempted people.

When they finally reached the promised land, the Hebrews were too intimidated by the size of the people who were dwelling there to challenge them for the land that was rightfully theirs. God punished their cowardice by sentencing them to wander in the wilderness another 40 years.

By the time Moses led them back, the entire generation of faithless Hebrews had died—except for the faithful spies Joshua and Caleb. Moses himself never entered the promised land, but just before he died he offered words of blessing, remembrance, inspiration, and encouragement to those who would enter (see Deut 33:1–34:8).

So ended an exceptional life.

For all of Moses' great accomplishments, perhaps the most significant and valuable are those that are glossed over in most retellings of his story. Think about the daily sacrifices he made for the sake of the Hebrew people. Think about the way he worked through his frustrations and fears, keeping the people in line without alienating them. Think about his passionate defense of the Hebrews when God was ready to destroy them (see Exod 32:7–14).

Moses lost his own opportunity to enter the promised land when he struck a rock in anger, disobeying God's command in the process (see Num 20:1–13). Yet still he persevered to ensure that others would reap what he could not.

THE TAKEAWAY

True greatness—the kind God recognizes and blesses—is achieved through daily faithfulness. True greatness isn't dramatic or showy; it doesn't call attention to itself. True greatness is built slowly over time. It comes from putting other people's needs first and sacrificing your own desires for God's greater good. It comes from maintaining a close relationship with the Lord and recognizing—and doing—his will.

Moses found himself at the center of some of the most dramatic events in Old Testament history. Yet his legacy is built on the fact that he helped God's people get where they needed to be. He sacrificed, endured, and used his God-given abilities for the sake of others. That's how Moses, who was born into greatness and had greatness thrust upon him, achieved greatness in God's eyes.

FOOD FOR THOUGHT

1. Think of someone you know who shows greatness, even if it's not obvious to most other people. What are the qualities you admire in that person?

2. To what kind of greatness might God be calling you?

3. What specific steps will you need to take in order to answer his call?

29

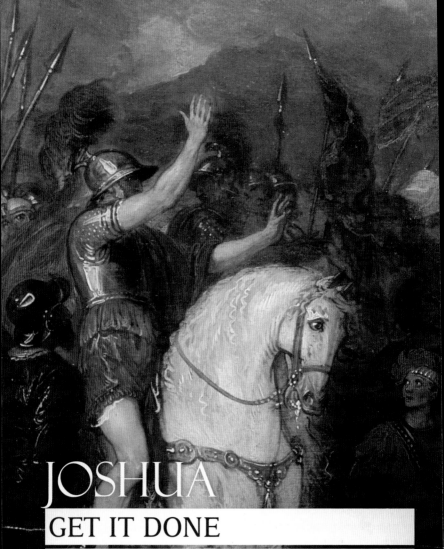

JOSHUA

GET IT DONE

"On that day the Lord exalted Joshua in the sight of all Israel, and they revered him throughout his life, as they had revered Moses." — Joshua 4:14

After Moses' death, the Hebrews needed a can-do leader to take them into the promised land—someone who understood the enormity of the task and wouldn't shrink from it.

They needed Joshua, one of the 12 spies Moses had sent to scout the land of Canaan. The spies had all returned with glowing reports about the rich bounty they saw in the land "flowing with milk and honey" (Num 13:27). But 10 of the spies warned Moses and the Israelites not to try to conquer the people who occupied the land, who were "giants" living in walled cities.

Joshua was not one of those faithless 10. He (along with a spy named Caleb) urged the Israelites to attack immediately. Their reasoning? The Israelites had God on their side. Unfortunately, Joshua and Caleb were overruled. The Israelites allowed their fears to get the best of them and refused to enter the land. As a result, they were forced to go back into the wilderness for 40 years, until the faithless generation died.

Forty years later, Joshua maintained the same can-do attitude displayed previously. Those four wasted decades in the wilderness had strengthened his resolve to trust God and to act immediately when an opportunity presented itself. And that made Joshua the kind of leader the Hebrew people needed. What's more, in that time Joshua had the opportunity to observe Moses' leadership style for 40 years, to learn from his mentor's successes and failures.

When the time came for entering the promised land, Joshua embraced his responsibilities—not only as the commander of the people and the army, but also as God's representative. He made sure the Israelites followed God's instructions precisely. And with great purposefulness, Joshua led the people across the Jordan River into the land God had promised their ancestors. To remind his people of his power and presence, the Lord parted the waters of the Jordan River so they could cross on dry land, just as the previous generation had done with Moses at the Red Sea.

The Israelites, once too frightened to step foot in the land, prepared themselves to follow Joshua into battle and fight for what was theirs. Their first destination was the walled city of Jericho.

God sent the commander of his heavenly army to meet Joshua just outside Jericho. He gave Joshua very specific—and very unusual—battle instructions. Once a day for six days the Israelites were to march around the perimeter of the city in complete silence. On the seventh day, they were to march around it seven times. The seventh time around, seven priests were to blow trumpets and all the people were to shout.

Joshua followed the instructions carefully. When the trumpets sounded and the people shouted, the walls of Jericho collapsed and the Israelites laid waste to the city and its inhabitants.

With their initial victory, though, came a hard-earned lesson. God had forbidden the Israelites to take spoils from Jericho. However, one Israelite warrior named Achan couldn't resist pocketing some souvenirs before he left the city.

The Israelites' next stop was the sparsely populated city of Ai, a place ripe for conquering. In a stunning turn of events, however, the people of Ai routed the Israelites, killing 36 of them in the process. The Israelites were devastated. Joshua beseeched God to explain the defeat. When God told him the nation was being punished because one person had violated his command, Joshua sprang into action. As per the Lord's instructions, he investigated every person from every family from every clan in Israel. Achan was found guilty. Joshua ordered Achan to be executed, along with his entire family—a drastic punishment, to be sure, but one that proved Joshua took God's commands seriously.

Joshua returned to Ai with his army and destroyed the city using an ambush strategy laid out by God himself. From there he led the Israelites to victories throughout the land.

When Israel's first battles ended, Joshua oversaw the distribution of land to the various tribes of Israel. He parceled out real estate according to God's instructions, just as he had done with every other leadership responsibility he'd been given. The Israelites expected nothing less from the man who had led them into the promised land.

In his old age, Joshua—and all of Israel—enjoyed a time of peace. Perhaps it was a gift from God for a job well done. Even today, Joshua is recognized as one of the greatest leaders in Jewish history.

THE TAKEAWAY

Enormous tasks are accomplished—and lasting legacies are built—through individual acts of obedience. Joshua wasn't intimidated by the enormity of his responsibilities. He trusted God to lead him one step—and one battle—at a time.

When a problem arose, Joshua addressed it immediately. When a victory was won, he gave praise to God and moved forward. He kept fighting the battles that needed to be fought until he had accomplished everything the Lord had set before him. In so doing, he set an example for all Christian leaders.

FOOD FOR THOUGHT

1. What seems the most overwhelming task in your life right now?

2. What advice might Joshua offer for making that task more manageable?

3. What specifically do you need to pray for regarding your tasks and responsibilities?

33

GIDEON

WHO, ME?

"This is nothing less than the sword of Gideon son of Joash, the Israelite. God has handed the entire Midianite camp over to him." — Judges 7:14

ideon was threshing grain in a wine press, to hide it from the marauding Midianites, when an angel of the Lord appeared to him and said, "The LORD is with you, mighty warrior" (Judg 6:12).

Gideon's initial reaction to the angel speaks volumes about Israel's misery at that time. For seven years, the Midianites, a ruthless band of desert dwellers, had terrorized God's people. They destroyed the Israelites' crops and livestock and laid waste to their land.

So when God's messenger suddenly appeared to him, Gideon didn't recoil in fear. He wasn't filled with joy, either. And it seems he didn't notice the title by which the angel addressed him. Instead, he seized on the angel's first five words.

If the Lord is with us, Gideon asked, *why has he handed us over to the Midianites?*

The angel assured Gideon that God was, at that moment, raising up a military leader to deliver Israel from the ravaging Midianites. And that mighty warrior was Gideon himself.

Gideon's response reflects disbelief. "Please, Lord, how can I deliver Israel? Look, my family is the weakest in Manasseh, and I am the youngest in my father's house" (Judg 6:15). Gideon had no credentials, no experience, and no standing in the Israelite community. He was about as unlikely a military leader as you'll ever find—but none of that mattered.

Gideon made the mistake that many people make when God calls them to action. He believed success depended on the one being called instead of on the One doing the calling. God quieted Gideon's concerns with six simple words: "But I will be with you" (Judg 6:16).

Gideon still needed more convincing. He asked God to confirm his calling—and to prove his might—with a conspicuous sign. Gideon left a fleece on the ground overnight and asked God to make the evening dew settle only on the fleece, leaving the ground around it dry. The next morning, the fleece was soaked and the ground was dry.

Pushing his luck a bit, Gideon asked the Lord for one more conspicuous display of power. He left the fleece out overnight again. This time, though, Gideon asked the Lord to leave the fleece dry when the overnight dew settled over the rest of the land. The next morning, the ground was soaked and the fleece was dry.

Convinced, Gideon assembled an army of 32,000 men and went out to engage the Midianites and their allies in battle. At that point the

Lord came to Gideon with another message: "You have too many people for Me to hand the Midianites over to you, or else Israel might brag: 'I did it myself.' Now announce in the presence of the people: 'Whoever is fearful and trembling may turn back and leave Mount Gilead'" (Judg 7:2–3).

Twenty-two thousand men disqualified themselves on account of fear and trembling, leaving 10,000 to do battle against a fighting force described as being as innumerable as a "swarm of locusts" (Judg 7:12).

But God wasn't finished. He ordered Gideon to pare down his army even more, based on the way his men drank water from a stream. When the paring was done, Gideon was left with only 300 men. God said that was enough, and Gideon believed him.

He divided his men into three companies and equipped each soldier with a trumpet and a pitcher concealing a lighted torch. They sneaked into the Midianite camp under cover of darkness. At Gideon's signal, the men blew their trumpets and smashed their pitchers.

The Midianites panicked. In the wild melee that followed, they attacked one another before fleeing in terror. Gideon and his men gave chase until they were finally able to end the Midianite threat once and for all. Thousands of Midianites fell to God's force of Gideon and his 300 men.

Gideon returned from the battle a national hero. The Israelites begged him to rule over them as king. Even in victory, though, Gideon knew his place. "I will not rule over you, and my son will not rule over you; the Lord will rule over you" (Judg 8:23).

THE TAKEAWAY

Humble readiness is the ideal default mode for God's people. The humble part comes from recognizing and acknowledging that you've done nothing to earn a role in God's plan. Gideon's genuine surprise at being called by God is the benchmark of a humble spirit.

The readiness part comes from recognizing and acknowledging that God is able to use anyone at any time to accomplish his will. Here, too, Gideon set an example. Once he became convinced that God had chosen him, he operated with a boldness that must have stunned those who knew him well. Gideon understood that he wasn't depending on his own prowess but on God's power. And suddenly the lines between what could and couldn't be accomplished were erased in his mind.

FOOD FOR THOUGHT

1. How has God used you in ways you never imagined?

2. Why is it so difficult to maintain a spirit of humility?

3. What's the best strategy for maintaining a spirit of readiness?

SAMSON

STRONG AND WEAK

"You will conceive and give birth to a son. You must never cut his hair, because the boy will be a Nazirite to God from birth, and he will begin to save Israel from the power of the Philistines." — Judges 13:5

hose who don't learn from history are doomed to repeat it. Those words would have made a good motto for Israel during its period of the judges. The seemingly endless cycle in which the Israelites found themselves went like this: The people of Israel would rebel against God, so God would allow their enemies—often the Philistines—to mistreat them. After several decades of oppression, the Israelites would call out to God for help. Then God would send a judge—a military leader—to deliver them from their enemies. One of the last of these judges was Samson.

Like several other men in this book, Samson had an intriguing origin story. His mother, who had been unable to conceive, was visited by an angel of the Lord, who told her she would have a son. The boy would be a Nazirite—one set apart for God's service and bound by certain vows. He was to abstain from alcohol and unclean food. He was also forbidden to cut his hair. God would give him superhuman strength and bless his efforts to lead the Israelites against the Philistines.

Samson, however, proved to be an unpredictable leader. He was driven more by personal whims and desires than by any sense of God-given responsibility. Case in point: his decision to marry a Philistine woman. He saw the young woman once and went straight home to demand that his father and mother arrange for him to marry her.

On a whim, he made a bet with the 30 Philistine men in his wedding party that they couldn't answer a riddle. When they did, he had to give them 30 linen garments and 30 changes of clothes. To pay off the bet, Samson traveled to the Philistine city of Ashkelon, killed 30 men there, stripped off their clothing, and gave them to the winners.

When he returned to claim his bride, he discovered that she'd been given to another man in marriage. Overwhelmed by a desire for vengeance, Samson caught 300 foxes, tied their tails together, put torches between them, and released the creatures into the surrounding grain fields, vineyards, and olive groves.

Samson later killed 1,000 Philistines with the jawbone of a donkey. He gave credit for his unlikely victory to God. Samson must have recognized that God was working through his spur-of-the-moment passions and fits of rage to accomplish greater purposes for Israel.

Samson's most notorious passion involved a woman named Delilah. When the leaders of the Philistines got wind of it, they each promised to give her 1,100 pieces of silver if she could get Samson to reveal the source of his strength. Their plan was to use Samson's passion against him.

Three times Delilah begged him to tell her his secret, and three times Samson lied to her. The Philistine officials grew desperate. Delilah pouted, pleaded, and prodded until Samson finally revealed to her that his strength would leave if ever his hair were shaved.

Delilah sent for the Philistine officials while Samson fell asleep on her lap. When he awoke, his hair was gone, along with his strength. The Philistines seized him, gouged out his eyes, and forced him to grind grain in prison.

Some time later the Philistines were celebrating their victory over their once-fearsome enemy. They demanded that Samson be brought to the temple to entertain them. They wanted to gloat in the presence of the once-mighty warrior brought low by his own uncontrollable passions.

No one seemed to notice that Samson's hair had grown back or suspect that his God might empower him again.

While thousands of Philistines celebrated around him, Samson prayed. He asked God to give him strength one more time. Then he placed his hands on the pillars that supported the idolatrous temple and pushed with all his might. The temple collapsed, killing him and thousands of his enemies.

A final victory for a mighty warrior or a sad end to a wasted life? Regardless of where you stand on the issue, you must acknowledge that Samson's story begs the question, what if . . . ?

What if Samson had been better able to control his desires? What if his passions had aligned more closely with God's will? What might he have accomplished as a focused leader of Israel?

THE TAKEAWAY

Uncontrolled or misdirected passion can bring down even the strongest person. Samson's extraordinary physical strength was no match for his obsession with Delilah, his thirst for vengeance on his enemies, and his love of a good time. Those passions distracted him from his responsibilities, alienated him from the people who cared most about him, and destroyed his life before he realized what was happening.

You can ensure that your passions don't become liabilities by periodically checking the alignment of your priorities. If you're passionate about the same things God is passionate about, he will work through you to accomplish his will. If your passions run in a different direction from God's, it's time for a realignment.

FOOD FOR THOUGHT

1. Which of your passions are most difficult to control or most easily misdirected?

2. How can you tell when your passions or priorities are starting to go awry?

3. What specific steps can you take to make sure your passions and priorities align with God's?

41

SAMUEL

HEED THE CALL

"Samuel grew, and the Lord was with him, and He fulfilled everything Samuel prophesied." — 1 Samuel 3:19

he circumstances that led to Samuel growing up in the tabernacle and receiving a unique call from God were unusual, even by biblical standards.

His mother, Hannah, had been unable to conceive. And in a culture that prized childbearing, barrenness was a devastating blow. To make matters worse, Hannah's husband had another wife who had given birth to several children and incessantly mocked Hannah for her glaring lack of offspring.

One day while she was visiting the tabernacle in Shiloh, Hannah poured her heart out to God. In anguish and despair, she begged the Lord to give her a son. In exchange, she vowed to give the boy back to God for his service, effectively waiving her right to raise her son.

God answered her desperate plea. Hannah conceived and gave birth to Samuel. True to her vow, Hannah took her son to Shiloh as soon as he was weaned. She left him in the care of Eli, the elderly high priest. Samuel became a Nazirite, one who was wholly devoted to God's service.

One evening, young Samuel was lying down in the tabernacle of the Lord when he heard a voice call to him. Samuel got up and ran to the room of Eli, the high priest. Samuel answered dutifully, "Here I am; you called me" (1 Sam 3:4).

"'I didn't call,' Eli replied. 'Go back and lie down'" (1 Sam 3:5).

As soon as Samuel obeyed, he heard the voice a second time. Again he quickly went to Eli's room and again he was told that Eli hadn't called him. Samuel lay back down, and the voice spoke yet again.

The third time Samuel went to Eli's room that fateful evening, the high priest finally realized what was happening—and whose voice was speaking. He gave Samuel specific instructions about how to respond the next time he heard the voice.

The chance to put his advice into practice came almost immediately after Samuel went back to bed.

"The LORD came, stood there, and called as before, 'Samuel, Samuel!'" (1 Sam 3:10).

The boy responded exactly as Eli had instructed him: "Speak, for Your servant is listening."

Those six words transformed Samuel's life. In the decades that followed, Samuel emerged as a rare "triple threat"—one who served God publicly as a priest, a prophet, and a judge—all because of the humble willingness to serve embodied in his reply to God's call.

Samuel did three things right that evening. First, he heard God's call and responded to it. He didn't recognize it at first, but he *heard* it. The conditions were certainly right for tuning in to God. Samuel lay in stillness. He had no distractions, no clatter of daily life, no background noise competing for his attention. When the voice came, he listened and reacted. He sensed that there was an opportunity for him to serve.

Second, he consulted a trusted spiritual adviser. Unsure of what more he could do, Samuel sought guidance from someone with more wisdom and experience in such matters. The advice Eli offered seemed sound to him, so he followed it.

Third, he approached God with a spirit of humility and obedience. By referring to himself as a servant, Samuel acknowledged his position and his role. A servant has no authority, no power, no personal agenda to carry out. A servant's job is to follow his master's instructions. Samuel was content—even eager—to serve God in any capacity.

At that moment, in the quiet of the tabernacle, Samuel couldn't have imagined what God had in store for him. But he soon discovered that God rewards faithful servants with greater and greater responsibilities. Years later, when Saul was chosen to rule as the first king of Israel, it was Samuel who anointed him (see 1 Sam 10:1). When the time came to choose Saul's successor, it was Samuel who (with God's prompting) looked past the youthfulness and unremarkable role of the youngest son of Jesse to find the godliness, as well as the warrior's mentality, within. It was Samuel who informed young David that one day he would be king (see 1 Samuel 16).

When Samuel died, the entire nation of Israel mourned for him (see 1 Sam 25:1)—a fitting tribute to a prophet, priest, judge, and humble servant of God.

THE TAKEAWAY

Samuel's legacy is built on one crucial decision: he submitted completely and unhesitatingly to God's call. He didn't understand it fully. He didn't know where it would lead. But he made obedience the number one priority in his life.

Samuel had the courage to answer God's call, the faith to trust the Lord with his life, and the selflessness to give up his own ambitions and desires for the sake of God's plan. Perhaps that's why God used him in such a powerful way.

Anyone looking to be used similarly is well-advised to look to Samuel's example.

FOOD FOR THOUGHT

1. What circumstances, ordinary or extraordinary, have put you in the position you're in right now?

2. What is God calling you to do?

3. What obstacles might make it difficult for you to respond to God's call as Samuel did?

SAUL

WRESTLING WITH DEMONS

"Now the Spirit of the Lord had left Saul, and an evil spirit sent from the Lord began to torment him." — 1 Samuel 16:14

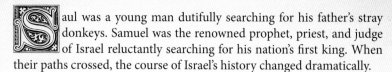aul was a young man dutifully searching for his father's stray donkeys. Samuel was the renowned prophet, priest, and judge of Israel reluctantly searching for his nation's first king. When their paths crossed, the course of Israel's history changed dramatically.

Samuel had served as the Lord's representative leader of Israel for decades, but he was growing old. When his sons proved to be unfit to succeed him, the people of Israel demanded that a king be appointed to rule over them. They were envious of the monarchies common in surrounding nations.

God warned the people that a king would take their sons to serve in his military and take their land, crops, flocks, and livestock for his own use. The Israelites were unmoved. They wanted a king, regardless of the consequences. So God obliged them.

God told Samuel that he would encounter Saul, whose only apparent qualification for kingship seems to have been that he was a head taller than most people. When Samuel anointed Saul as king, the people of Israel got what they wanted—for better or worse.

For someone with no previous experience—and no inkling that he would ever become royalty—Saul started strong. When the city of Jabesh-gilead came under siege by the Ammonites, Saul raised an army of 330,000 men and led them to victory (see 1 Samuel 11).

Unfortunately, that example of heroic leadership proved the exception rather than the rule of Saul's reign. Instead of wrestling with the problems facing the nation of Israel, Saul spent most of his time wrestling with his own personal problems.

He wrestled first with insecurity. Despite the fact that he stood head and shoulders above most people, Saul struggled with self-esteem issues. When the time came for Samuel to introduce him publicly as God's choice for Israel's first king, Saul was nowhere to be found. Searchers eventually discovered him hiding behind some supplies (see 1 Sam 10:21–23). Rather than embrace his calling, Saul ran from it.

Saul also wrestled with jealousy—specifically, jealousy of David. The tone was set early in their relationship. Saul wasn't on the battlefield the day David killed the giant Goliath. It could be argued that David did Saul's job for him that day. As the tall commander in chief of Israel's army, Saul should have been the one to face Goliath.

When the victorious Israelite army returned home from the battle, people gathered beside the road to cheer them. Some of the more boisterous ones sang, "Saul has killed his thousands, but David his tens of thousands"

(1 Sam 18:7). Those words triggered something in the king, and he became obsessed with destroying David.

Saul appointed David to be his court musician, to play his harp when Saul's spirit needed soothing. He gave David his daughter's hand in marriage. Yet Saul also lived with the knowledge that he was a lame-duck monarch. Shortly into his reign, God effectively took the kingdom from him because of his disobedience.

Saul also suspected that David would be his eventual successor. And though David showed nothing but complete loyalty to the king, Saul despised him. In fact, on more than one occasion, his jealousy reached such a fever pitch that Saul tried to murder David personally.

Finally, and most devastatingly, Saul wrestled with depression. His relationship with the Lord had deteriorated over the years as a result of his many harmful and destructive decisions as king. When his own personal darkness began to envelop him, he found himself unable to turn to the only One who could help.

In desperation, he visited a medium, a practitioner of dark arts (see 1 Samuel 28). He asked her to bring forth the spirit of Samuel, who had recently died. Samuel's spirit made it clear that

- the kingdom of Israel had been taken from Saul for good;

- the Israelites would fall to the Philistines in battle the next day; and

- neither Saul nor his sons would live to see the end of that battle.

Even from beyond the grave, Samuel's prophecies proved unassailable. The next day, after watching his sons die in battle, Saul was gravely wounded by Philistine archers. Rather than allowing his injuries to run their course, Saul chose to take matters into his own hands one last time. He threw himself on his own sword and died (see 1 Samuel 31).

With this final desperate act, Saul secured his legacy of squandered potential. In his insecurity, jealousy, and depression, he lashed out at the people closest to him and alienated those committed to helping him succeed and thrive as king of Israel, including God himself.

THE TAKEAWAY

Emotional demons are real, and they can be devastating. Saul neglected to deal healthily with his very real emotional struggles. As a result, he lost his joy, his sense of purpose, and eventually his life.

FOOD FOR THOUGHT

1. When was the last time you allowed an emotional struggle to get the better of you? What were the results?

2. Why is it sometimes difficult to seek God's help when you're in the midst of an emotional battle?

3. How can you specifically help someone who is struggling emotionally?

DAVID

A MAN LOYAL TO GOD

"After removing [Saul], He raised up David as their king and testified about him: 'I have found David the son of Jesse, a man loyal to Me, who will carry out all My will.'"
—Acts 13:22

s epithets go, it's hard to beat God's description of David in the book of Acts: "a man loyal to [God]." A glimpse into David's life reveals what it takes to be awarded such a designation.

First, a man who is loyal to God understands God's power. David didn't challenge the giant Goliath to prove his own toughness; he did it to prove God's strength. He came upon a scene in which no one else among God's people seemed to grasp who was backing them.

The Philistine warrior Goliath taunted the Israelite forces and slandered their God. David expected one of the Israelites to step forward and, with the power of God behind him, end the Philistine's reign of terror. Instead, he found a group of men too intimidated by Goliath's size and threats to do anything.

Since he was the only one who could see which side actually had the overwhelming advantage, young David volunteered to face Goliath. King Saul tried to outfit David with his armor and sword, but David respectfully declined them. Traditional gear had no place in this confrontation. The battle would be fought using God's power.

As he walked boldly onto the battlefield to face the heavily armored and armed Philistine behemoth, David scooped up five rocks, pulled out his trusty sling, and said to Goliath, "You come against me with a dagger, spear, and sword, but I come against you in the name of Yahweh of Hosts, the God of Israel's armies—you have defied Him. Today, the LORD will hand you over to me" (1 Sam 17:45–46). And with one shot, he felled the giant.

Second, a man who is loyal to God acts according to God's timing. David had been anointed the future king of Israel when he was a young man. For years he knew he was destined to succeed Saul. Yet he never allowed a personal pursuit of the throne to override God's plans.

David had to flee for his life from Saul. He spent years on the run, hiding from the king and his men. However, because he was a cunning warrior, he often turned the tables on his pursuers. First Samuel 24 records an occasion in which Saul, while chasing David, stopped to relieve himself. The cave he chose as his restroom just happened to be David's hiding place.

Seeing Saul in such a vulnerable position, David's men urged him to sneak up on the murderous king and end his life. David refused, saying, "I swear before the LORD: I would never do such a thing to my lord, the LORD's anointed" (1 Sam 24:6). The man had tried to kill David on several occasions, yet David refused to raise his hand against him because God had not condoned it.

David eventually became king of Israel, but it happened according to God's timing, not his.

Third, a man who is loyal to God feels his sin deeply. David was still a flawed human, capable of stunningly bad decisions and precipitous falls from grace.

One evening David spotted a woman taking a bath on a nearby rooftop. The woman was Bathsheba, the wife of Uriah, one of David's most loyal soldiers, who was away at war. David sent for Bathsheba and started an affair with her. Shortly thereafter, Bathsheba became pregnant.

David immediately sent for Uriah. He reasoned that Uriah would come home and sleep with his wife. When the baby was born some nine months later, then, everyone would assume that Uriah was the father.

But Uriah's loyalty got in the way of David's plan. Uriah refused to lie with his wife while his fellow soldiers were still fighting. So David switched to Plan B. He arranged for Uriah to be abandoned during battle and killed by Israel's enemies. After Uriah's death, David married Bathsheba to make their baby seem legitimate.

But God knew what he had done and allowed the baby boy to die as punishment for David's sin. David was crushed.

More acute than the grief he felt over the loss of his son or the guilt over what he'd done to Uriah or the humiliation he'd brought on himself was the devastation he felt over what he'd done to his relationship with God. David poured out his feelings in Psalm 51: "Wash away my guilt and cleanse me from my sin. For I am conscious of my rebellion, and my sin is always before me. Against You—You alone—I have sinned and done this evil in Your sight" (vv. 2–4).

Those are the words of a man loyal to God.

THE TAKEAWAY

Understanding who God is and what he wants from you can be found in reading his Word and pursuing a rich prayer life. By making those things a priority, you can begin to develop a deeper relationship with God and grow in your loyalty to him.

FOOD FOR THOUGHT

1. Read Psalm 51. What do David's words tell you about his relationship with God?

2. What's the difference between David's relationship with God and yours?

3. What steps can you take to submit to God's timing in your life?

NATHAN

SPEAKING TRUTH TO POWER

"So the Lord sent Nathan to David." — 2 Samuel 12:1

It's one thing to speak the truth to people in power when you have nothing to lose. It's quite another to speak the truth when you have *everything* to lose. The Old Testament prophet Nathan faced the prospect of losing everything, including his life, if he spoke the truth to the most powerful man in Israel. Yet that was exactly what God called him to do.

Nathan served as the court prophet of King David. He relayed messages from the Lord and acted as a spiritual adviser to the king. Nothing in his experience, however, prepared him for the assignment God gave him in 2 Samuel 12.

God sent Nathan to confront David about his adulterous affair with a woman named Bathsheba. Nathan had no way of knowing how David would react to such a confrontation. After all, David was not just the king; he was also a skilled warrior. He had a warrior's mentality. He also had legions of dangerous men ready to do whatever he asked. One word from him could mean death to anyone who displeased him.

Uriah discovered that truth the hard way. Uriah was Bathsheba's soldier husband, who was away at war when the king began his affair with Bathsheba. When Bathsheba's pregnancy threatened to reveal the affair, David desperately looked for a way to avoid a public scandal.

The plan he eventually settled on required that he arrange to have Uriah killed in battle. That way, David could quickly marry the widowed Bathsheba and establish a plausible—and acceptable—timeline for her pregnancy. No one would be the wiser.

Except Nathan.

Surely the thought crossed Nathan's mind that if David had been willing to kill one of his most loyal soldiers in order to cover up his transgression, he wouldn't hesitate to do the same to a nosy prophet.

But Nathan would not be dissuaded from his task. His concern wasn't for his safety but for the effectiveness of his presentation. He had one chance to speak God's truth to someone who desperately needed to hear it, and he was determined to give his best to the effort.

Nathan didn't barge in to the king's palace, shouting accusations and demanding repentance. He didn't publicly shame or embarrass David. He didn't antagonize him by listing the many ways he'd failed his people.

Instead, Nathan told David a parable about a rich man who owned many sheep and cattle and a poor man who owned only one ewe lamb. The poor man loved the lamb dearly and treated it as a family member. He shared his food with the lamb and let it drink from his cup and sleep in his arms.

One day a traveler arrived at the rich man's house. As was the custom of the day, the rich man entertained his guest by preparing a lavish meal. But he couldn't bring himself to use one of his own sheep or cattle for the feast. So he took the poor man's lamb, killed it, and served it to his guest.

To say that Nathan's story had its intended effect would be an understatement. Second Samuel 12:5–10 picks up the account from there.

> David was infuriated with the man and said to Nathan: "As the LORD lives, the man who did this deserves to die! Because he has done this thing and shown no pity, he must pay four lambs for that lamb."
>
> Nathan replied to David, "You are the man! This is what the LORD God of Israel says: 'I anointed you king over Israel, and I delivered you from the hand of Saul. I gave your master's house to you and your master's wives into your arms, and I gave you the house of Israel and Judah, and if that was not enough, I would have given you even more. Why then have you despised the command of the LORD by doing what I consider evil? You struck down Uriah the Hittite with the sword and took his wife as your own wife—you murdered him with the Ammonite's sword. Now therefore, the sword will never leave your house because you despised Me and took the wife of Uriah the Hittite to be your own wife.'"

Nathan's boldness and creativity caused David to recognize the gravity of his sin and to repent. Nathan spoke the truth to a person in power without worrying about the repercussions—and he did so in a way that would have great impact. That's why his story stands as an inspiration and an example to be followed by God's people today.

THE TAKEAWAY

Simply speaking God's truth, whether it's to someone in power or someone you've known your entire life, isn't enough. Your responsibility is to speak his truth in a way that resonates with your audience. The right message delivered in the wrong way will likely fall on deaf ears or cause hearts to harden. The right message delivered in the right way can change lives.

FOOD FOR THOUGHT

1. What are some of the risks of speaking God's truth, whether it's to people in power or people you know?

2. What are some mistakes you've made when it comes to speaking God's truth to others? What did you learn from your mistakes?

3. What is the best strategy for speaking God's truth in a given situation?

SOLOMON

GET WISDOM

"I will therefore do what you have asked. I will give you a wise and understanding heart, so that there has never been anyone like you before and never will be again." — 1 Kings 3:12

Shortly after Bathsheba's son Solomon succeeded his father, David, as king of Israel, God appeared to him in a dream. In it, the Lord made him an offer unprecedented in Scripture. Anything Solomon requested—wealth, long life, revenge on his enemies—God would grant him.

And Solomon replied, "You have shown great and faithful love to Your servant, my father David, because he walked before You in faithfulness, righteousness, and integrity. You have continued this great and faithful love for him by giving him a son to sit on his throne, as it is today.

"Lord my God, You have now made Your servant king in my father David's place. Yet I am just a youth with no experience in leadership. Your servant is among Your people You have chosen, a people too numerous to be numbered or counted. So give Your servant an obedient heart to judge Your people and to discern between good and evil. For who is able to judge this great people of Yours?" (1 Kgs 3:6–9)

For all of Solomon's noteworthy accomplishments, the most awe-inspiring thing he ever did was to utter those words. They not only set the course for the rest of his life but also revealed three vital truths about wisdom (or discernment) that still apply today.

First, the selfless pursuit of wisdom pleases God. Solomon asked for wisdom—the ability to discern between good and evil and to judge fairly—not for his own ego, but for the sake of God's people. He wanted to be a godly leader.

God granted Solomon's request by giving him a "wise and understanding heart"—perhaps the wisest and most understanding human heart that ever beat. But that's not all. God was so pleased with Solomon's request that he gave him untold riches and honor as well. On top of his unsurpassed wisdom, Solomon became one of the richest and most renowned people in history.

Second, wisdom is highly valued by other people. The first great test of Solomon's wisdom came when two prostitutes approached him with a seemingly unsolvable dispute. The two women lived together and both had recently given birth to sons.

One night one of the babies died in his sleep. When his mother discovered his lifeless body, she quickly switched babies with the other mother, who was still sleeping. That woman, after an initial panic upon awaking, realized the lifeless baby was not her son. So both women appeared before Solomon, claiming to be the mother of the living infant.

Solomon ordered that baby to be cut in half with a sword and given to both women. At his words, one of the women immediately renounced her claim to the boy and pleaded with Solomon to give him (unharmed) to her rival. The other woman urged Solomon to carry out his plan. Instead, Solomon ordered the baby to be given to the first woman, who had shown a mother's compassion. When the people of Israel heard about Solomon's decision, "they stood in awe of the king because they saw that God's wisdom was in him to carry out justice" (1 Kgs 3:28). Word of his wisdom spread throughout the surrounding nations as well (see 1 Kgs 4:34).

Third, when the pursuit of wisdom is abandoned, bad things happen. With fame and fortune come many temptations. The highly developed thought processes that marked Solomon's public persona seem to have abandoned him in his private life.

He took more than 700 wives and 300 concubines, many of them from foreign, idol-worshipping nations. Over time, their influence turned Solomon's heart away from God. He engaged in idol worship and disobeyed God's commands, until God finally tore the kingdom of Israel away—not from Solomon himself, but from his sons.

The reign that started with such potential and promise turned out to be the beginning of the end of the united kingdom of Israel—all because Solomon abandoned his pursuit of wisdom.

THE TAKEAWAY

Like Solomon, you have the option of pursuing wealth, long life, or wisdom—not to mention fame, comfort, entertainment, and security.

Strong cases can be made for the value of each option. Yet as Solomon's story demonstrates, wisdom is always the best choice. Wisdom allows you to apply what you know in ways that benefit you and others (and not necessarily in that order). Wisdom helps you understand and apply

Scripture. Wisdom allows you to use your God-given gifts in extraordinary ways.

God rewards the pursuit of wisdom. He may not lavish you with wealth and fame, as he did Solomon, but he will allow you to experience such intangible perks as peace of mind, security, and respect.

Since God is the source of all wisdom, a close relationship with him and his Word is essential in the pursuit of wisdom. The more you understand about what God desires—what pleases and displeases him—the better equipped you'll be to make wise decisions.

FOOD FOR THOUGHT

1. When was the last time you demonstrated God-honoring wisdom? When was the last time you wish you'd shown God-honoring wisdom?

2. What difference can wisdom make—in your life and in the lives of others?

3. What's the best strategy for becoming a wiser person?

ELIJAH

SOLO, BUT NOT ALONE

"At the time for offering the evening sacrifice, Elijah the prophet approached the altar and said, 'Yahweh, God of Abraham, Isaac, and Israel, today let it be known that You are God in Israel and I am Your servant, and that at Your word I have done all these things. Answer me, Lord! Answer me so that this people will know that you, Yahweh, are God and that You have turned their hearts back.'" — 1 Kings 18:36–37

s a prophet of God in Israel during the reign of King Ahab and Queen Jezebel, Elijah was an endangered species. The evil royal couple had done everything in their power to rid the nation of God's spokespeople so that their own prophets of the false gods Baal and Asherah could do their work unopposed.

Elijah had a target on his back because he had announced God's judgment on Israel. A devastating drought gripped the land, wreaking havoc on the nation's food and water supply. Missing the point of judgment completely, King Ahab blamed *Elijah* for the drought (see 1 Kgs 18:17).

Elijah refused to be cowed. Prompted by God, he challenged the 450 prophets of Baal and the 400 prophets of Asherah to a winner-take-all contest. The rules were simple. Two sacrificial altars would be built: one to the Lord God and one to Baal. The first deity to send fire to accept his sacrifice would be declared the God of Israel.

On the appointed day, the prophets of Baal assembled at Mount Carmel to prepare their wood and altar, as well as the bull they intended to sacrifice. When everything was just so, they began to pray to their god to accept their sacrifice.

From morning until noon, they called out to Baal, begging and pleading with him to send a fire. They danced to get his attention and then shouted louder. When that didn't work, they cut themselves with knives and spears, hoping their blood would arouse Baal's interest. "All afternoon they kept on raving until the offering of the evening sacrifice, but there was no sound; no one answered, no one paid attention" (1 Kgs 18:29). The prophets of Baal failed to elicit even a slight warming of their sacrifice.

The eyes of the nation turned to Elijah, the sole representative of Yahweh, to see if he could accomplish what his Baal-worshipping opponents could not.

Elijah's first step was to repair the altar of the Lord that had been torn down in Israel's rush to embrace the idols and false gods of their neighbors. He used 12 stones to represent the 12 tribes of Israel.

His next step was to dig a trench, deep enough to hold four gallons of water, around the altar. He covered the top of the altar with firewood, cut up his bull for sacrifice, and placed the meat on top of the wood.

With everything in place, there was only one more preparation to be made. Elijah handed out four large water pots and instructed people to fill them with water and pour it over his sacrifice and altar—not once, not twice, but three times.

All told, 12 pots of water were poured over Elijah's sacrifice, drenching the meat, the wood, and the altar itself. The runoff filled the surrounding trench.

The onlookers—including the exhausted and bloodied prophets of Baal—must have been stunned by Elijah's strategy. He'd made it practically impossible for anything to ignite his sacrifice.

And that was precisely his intent.

Elijah approached his waterlogged altar and prayed aloud for everyone to hear: "Yahweh, God of Abraham, Isaac, and Israel, today let it be known that You are God in Israel and I am Your servant, and that at Your word I have done all these things. Answer me, LORD! Answer me so that this people will know that You, Yahweh, are God and that You have turned their hearts back" (1 Kgs 18:36–37).

Fire descended from heaven to devour Elijah's offering, along with the wood beneath it, the stones of the altar, and the dirt on which the altar was built. The flames even consumed every drop of water in the trench that surrounded the altar.

The Lord sent an unmistakable message to his people about what the living God is capable of—and why false gods should be dismissed as the nonentities they are. The impact was immediate and profound. "When all the people saw it, they fell facedown and said, 'Yahweh, He is God! Yahweh, He is God!'" (1 Kgs 18:39).

The Lord also sent a message to believers throughout the ages about what one person who fully trusts in him can accomplish.

THE TAKEAWAY

If you represent God and are doing his work, traditional ideas about what is or isn't possible have no relevance. No odds are too high, no opponent is too intimidating, and no obstacle is too extreme to overcome. The more deeply you cling to those truths, the more willing you'll be to take risks in your faith, as Elijah did.

FOOD FOR THOUGHT

1. When was the last time you took a solo stand—or what *felt* like a solo stand—for your spiritual beliefs?

2. What obstacles prevent believers from risking more in their faith?

3. What specific steps can you take to remove such obstacles from your own Christian journey?

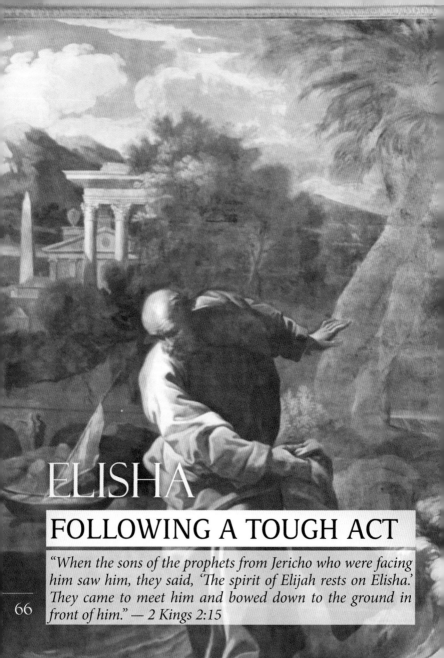

ELISHA

FOLLOWING A TOUGH ACT

"When the sons of the prophets from Jericho who were facing him saw him, they said, 'The spirit of Elijah rests on Elisha.' They came to meet him and bowed down to the ground in front of him." — 2 Kings 2:15

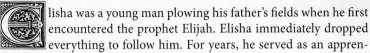

lisha was a young man plowing his father's fields when he first encountered the prophet Elijah. Elisha immediately dropped everything to follow him. For years, he served as an apprentice while Elijah performed his duties as a prophet—often under extreme circumstances. Elisha was privy to Elijah's personal highs and lows, to his courageous obedience and crippling doubts. He observed the way Elijah interacted with kings and commoners. He studied the prophet's personal relationship with God.

Elisha absorbed the example set by his mentor. Elijah's influence helped shape Elisha's spiritual outlook. And when the time came for Elijah to depart—via a whirlwind to heaven—Elisha was ready to assume his own role as a prophet of God.

It's telling that Elisha's first act after Elijah's departure was to use his mentor's mantle to part the waters of the Jordan River. Elijah's influence was obvious. Yet Elisha faced circumstances that Elijah never did. So while he was greatly influenced by his mentor's example, Elisha had to walk the unique path God had laid out for *him*.

His first test came when the people of Jericho approached him about a life-threatening situation. The water of the area was bad, causing sickness in humans and livestock and preventing vegetation from growing. Elisha instructed them to bring him a new bowl filled with salt. He poured the salt into a nearby spring and pronounced God's blessing on it. Immediately the water of the area became pure—sweet to the taste and highly effective for growing crops (see 2 Kgs 2:19–22).

Elisha was quickly reminded that where God's work is being done, there will be opposition. As he approached the town of Bethel, a group of boys gathered to hurl insults and verbal abuse at him. But in mocking Elisha—God's representative to his people—they were also mocking God. So God sent a couple of ferocious female bears from a nearby forest into the crowd of mockers, and the bears mauled 42 of them (see 2 Kgs 2:23–25). Needless to say, respect for Elisha and his work increased significantly after that.

When the kings of Israel, Judah, and Edom joined together to fight the Moabites, they turned to Elisha in a moment of crisis. On the verge of battle, their soldiers had no water to drink. Their extreme thirst made them weak and vulnerable. Elisha told the kings to dig ditches; there they would find pure drinking water for the soldiers and their horses. First, though, he rebuked the king of Israel—to his face—for the wickedness and idolatry that ran rampant in his kingdom. Elisha proclaimed

God's word boldly, with no fear for his own safety and with no concern for his future.

That partially explains why God used him to accomplish some remarkable feats. When the widow of one of the sons of God's prophets told Elisha that creditors were going to take her sons because of her husband's unpaid debts, Elisha gave her instructions that miraculously turned one small pot of oil into a surplus of oil that she was able to sell to pay those debts (see 2 Kgs 4:1–7).

When the young son of an elderly Shunammite couple suddenly died, Elisha prayed over the boy's body until God brought him back to life. When a military commander named Naaman was stricken by a skin disease, Elisha instructed him to dip himself in the Jordan River seven times in order to be healed. Naaman did as he was told and received God's healing.

During his 65 years of service, Elisha became a revered and beloved fixture among God's people. Like his mentor, Elijah, he was renowned for his fearlessness and faithfulness in serving the Lord. When he died, the entire nation of Israel mourned. Elisha had been schooled by one of the best; but ultimately his ministry, influence, and legacy were unlike anyone else's.

THE TAKEAWAY

God has equipped you with a unique set of skills and abilities. He has a unique path chosen for you. The circumstances you face, the opportunities you have to make a difference in other people's lives, and the specific calling you've been given by your heavenly Father are unlike any other. Your Christian journey is just that: *your* Christian journey.

One of the best ways to prepare for that journey is to observe the lives of other trusted, mature believers. Mentors are gifts from God. The things you learn from their successes and failures can have tremendous impact on your own Christian experience. With time—and a little seasoning—you can become a mentor to others.

FOOD FOR THOUGHT

1. Name the most influential Christians in your life up to this point. What specific lessons have you learned from each of them?

2. How has their influence shaped your own Christian walk, from the way you interact with others to the way you study Scripture?

3. If someone were to look to you as a mentor, what lessons could they gain from the relationship?

EZRA AND NEHEMIAH

DREAM BIG, WORK HARD

"So I said to them, 'You see the trouble we are in. Jerusalem lies in ruins and its gates have been burned down. Come, let's rebuild Jerusalem's wall, so that we will no longer be a disgrace.' I told them how the gracious hand of my God had been on me, and what the king had said to me.

"They said, 'Let's start rebuilding,' and they were encouraged to do this good work." — Nehemiah 2:17–18

ne of the hallmarks of God's relationship with the people of Israel was patience. He led them to the promised land despite their constant whining and complaining. He gave them the human monarchy they desired when they rejected him as king. He tempered his punishment when they turned their backs on him to pursue other gods—mere idols.

He gave his people ample warning of the judgment that was to come if they continued to reject him. He sent prophet after prophet to spell out what would happen to the kingdom if the people continued in their unrepentant ways.

But the Israelites were a hard-hearted bunch. They ignored God's prophets and shrugged off his dire warnings until it was too late.

When God's judgment came, it came hard. In 722 BC, he allowed the northern kingdom of Israel to fall to the Assyrians. Judgment for the southern kingdom of Judah came in the form of the Babylonians, who conquered the capital city of Jerusalem in 586 BC.

Conquered is perhaps too mild of a word for what the Babylonians did to the city. They laid waste to Jerusalem, leaving no structure undamaged. They destroyed Solomon's temple as well as the walls that surrounded and protected the city. For decades Jerusalem lay in ruins, a testament to God's judgment, while many of its citizens were held captive in Babylon (and later, Persia).

In captivity, the Israelites repented of their disobedience and begged God to restore their kingdom. God answered their prayers by softening the hearts of their captors. Around 536 BC, a man named Zerubbabel received permission from Cyrus, the king of Persia, to lead a group of Jewish exiles back to Jerusalem. Their goal was to rebuild the temple of Jerusalem, the center of worship for the Jewish people. Despite some opposition, the builders completed their work in about 20 years.

Two notable figures of the Old Testament drew inspiration from Zerubbabel's success and determined to build on it. Around 458 BC, a priest named Ezra approached the Persian king, Darius, to request permission to lead a second wave of Jewish exiles back to Jerusalem. Darius agreed to Ezra's request. The returnees were able to populate only a small section of their former homeland, but they were determined to change that.

Around 444 BC, a royal cupbearer named Nehemiah received word that the returnees were in grave danger because the walls of Jerusalem were still in ruins. The exiles had no protection from their enemies.

The news devastated Nehemiah, who immediately turned to God in fasting and prayer. King Artaxerxes of Persia recognized that something was wrong with his cupbearer and asked Nehemiah about it. When Nehemiah explained the situation, Artaxerxes gave him permission—and provisions—to lead another group of exiles back to Jerusalem to rebuild the city's walls.

Nehemiah's mission represented an enormous step in the reestablishing of Israel's national identity. It's little surprise, then, that he faced heavy opposition to his plan. The surrounding nations of Canaan were none too eager to see Israel's return to prominence. The proposed wall would give Jerusalem protection from attack and restore some of its military viability. It was in the national interest of the Samaritans, Ammonites, and Philistines to keep Jerusalem vulnerable.

Rumors of impending attacks did little to disrupt Nehemiah's construction schedule. Occasionally builders worked with a tool in one hand and a weapon in the other. Sanballat, the leader of the Samaritans, accused Nehemiah of plotting a rebellion against Persia. He even managed to convince certain Jewish nobles and prophets to oppose the project. Yet Nehemiah persevered and the construction continued. And in 54 days the walls were completed.

Israel eventually regained its identity as a nation because a handful of people dared to dream big and cared enough to do everything necessary to make that dream a reality.

THE TAKEAWAY

Perhaps the apostle Paul had the stories of Ezra and Nehemiah in mind when he wrote, "We know that all things work together for the good of those who love God: those who are called according to His purpose" (Rom 8:28). No situation is beyond the Lord's control, and no task

is too difficult for him. If he can cause pagan rulers and other unlikely allies to assist the Israelites in restoring their homeland, he can produce all kinds of unexpected blessings in the lives of his people.

The key to discovering what God is capable of is to

- be active in your faith;

- step outside your comfort zone; and

- recognize people's needs and step forward to address them.

FOOD FOR THOUGHT

1. If you were to dream big, as Ezra and Nehemiah did, what do you think God might accomplish in and through you?

2. What obstacles are standing in the way of those dreams?

3. What specific steps can you take to overcome those obstacles or lessen their influence in your life?

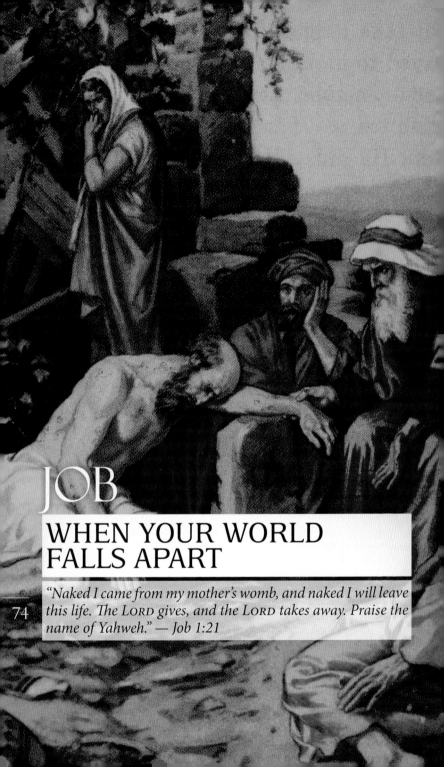

JOB

WHEN YOUR WORLD FALLS APART

"Naked I came from my mother's womb, and naked I will leave this life. The Lord gives, and the Lord takes away. Praise the name of Yahweh." — Job 1:21

f everything good in your life were suddenly taken away, what would you do? That question lies at the heart of Job's story in the Old Testament book bearing his name.

Job was a righteous man—someone so above reproach that God held him up to Satan as a model servant. Satan was unimpressed. "Of course Job is faithful to you," he countered. "He has wealth, family, and excellent health. Take away those things and let's see how faithful he is."

God agreed to Satan's challenge. He allowed the Devil to carry tragedy and suffering into Job's life. First came messengers with news that all of Job's flocks—the primary source of his wealth—had been stolen or killed. Suddenly Job was faced with the prospect of poverty.

Before he could gather his thoughts, though, he was dealt a more devastating blow. Another messenger arrived with news that a desert windstorm had collapsed the house of Job's oldest son, where all of Job's children had been celebrating. None of them made it out alive. Suddenly Job, who had been deeply involved in the lives of his sons and daughters, found himself childless.

Next came the theft of his camels and then boils. Job 2:7 says God allowed Satan to afflict Job with painful boils from the bottom of his feet to the top of his head. Job was in agony, emotionally and physically. Yet he maintained a faithful, humble, and obedient attitude toward God.

The general consensus, even among those closest to him, was that Job had done something to incur God's wrath. Job's protests of innocence fell on skeptical ears.

> His wife said to him, "Do you still retain your integrity? Curse God and die!"

> "You speak as a foolish woman speaks," he told her. "Should we accept only good from God and not adversity?" Throughout all this Job did not sin in what he said. (Job 2:9–10)

Three friends—Eliphaz, Bildad, and Zophar—arrived to comfort Job and were stunned by what they saw. Job's suffering had made him almost unrecognizable. For seven days the trio sat in a respectful silence with Job.

Job broke the vigil by suggesting that it would be preferable never to have been born than to experience the kind of pain and grief he was enduring. Eliphaz responded by reminding Job of the people he (Job) had comforted in the past. But then Eliphaz quickly pointed out: "But now that this has happened to you, you have become exhausted. It strikes you, and you are dismayed. Isn't your piety your confidence, and the integrity of your life your hope? Consider: who has perished when he was innocent? Where have the honest been destroyed?" (Job 4:5–7).

Like Job's wife, Eliphaz believed that Job's suffering was due to sin. He urged his friend to repent. Bildad and Zophar chimed in, instructing Job to be more blameless in his walk with God. But they didn't stop there. Bildad suggested that Job's children had brought their deaths on themselves. Zophar stated Job probably deserved even worse punishment for whatever it was he'd done.

Job countered these accusations, insisting once again that he was innocent before God. At the same time, he struggled mightily with his situation, trying to square his suffering with what he knew about God. In the depths of his despair, he posed some difficult questions about God's justice and humankind's inability to grasp his ways.

Job pleaded for someone to serve as a mediator between him and God, someone to represent him and get the answers that eluded him. At his lowest point, he begged God to send him to Sheol, the place of the dead (see Job 14:13).

Through it all, Job managed to hold on to his relationship with the Lord—at times by his fingernails, but he held on just the same. He committed himself to the pursuit of wisdom by fearing God and avoiding wickedness.

When Satan's period of testing was over, God rewarded Job's faithfulness. He restored Job's health and gave him a long life. He bestowed on Job more wealth and possessions than he'd had before his season of suffering. And he blessed Job with a new family—seven sons and three daughters.

Job walked the path through the valley of darkness and emerged with God's blessing on the other side.

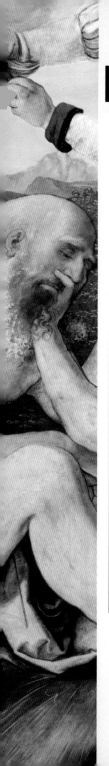

THE TAKEAWAY

Everyone faces seasons of loss, grief, and suffering. Instead of asking, "Why is this happening to me?" a better response is to ask, "How will I respond to this?" If you stay close to God when things get dark—that is, if you resist the urge to blame him or turn your back on him—you will find opportunities to grow and perhaps even thrive in the midst of your trials. You will also set a powerful example of faith in action for others.

FOOD FOR THOUGHT

1. Imagine that a loved one experiences extreme suffering or a sudden loss. What would you say to or do for that person?

2. What Bible passages or personal experiences would you use to back up your statements?

3. Describe a time when you saw God bring something good from a situation that seemed hopeless.

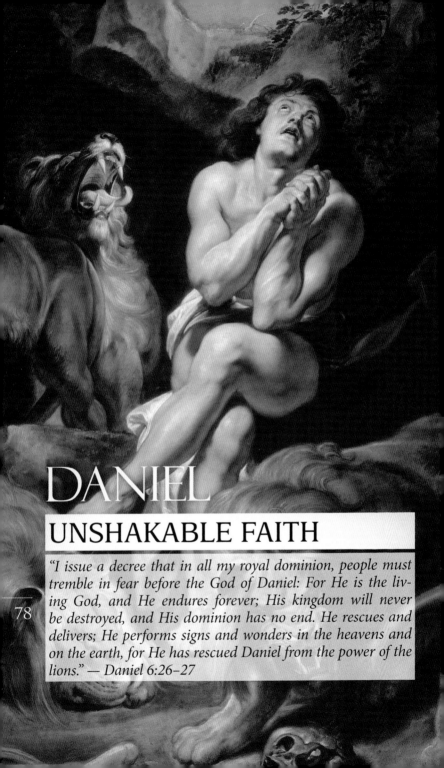

DANIEL

UNSHAKABLE FAITH

"I issue a decree that in all my royal dominion, people must tremble in fear before the God of Daniel: For He is the living God, and He endures forever; His kingdom will never be destroyed, and His dominion has no end. He rescues and delivers; He performs signs and wonders in the heavens and on the earth, for He has rescued Daniel from the power of the lions." — Daniel 6:26–27

rom a historical perspective, it seems that Daniel came of age at exactly the wrong time in Israel. He was born just in time to see his once-great nation fall to the Babylonians. As punishment for their centuries of unfaithfulness and disobedience, God allowed his people to be defeated by their enemies. Daniel, along with other young, strong, and capable people in Israel, was carried away into captivity in Babylon.

From a spiritual perspective, however, it's apparent that Daniel came of age at exactly the *right* time. During his years as a captive in Babylon, Daniel made a lasting impression on key figures in the Babylonian and (later) Persian governments. He revealed God's power and protectiveness in ways no one would forget.

Daniel was groomed for government service from the time of his capture. Under God's guiding hand, he made a name for himself as a wise and trusted adviser to King Nebuchadnezzar. His later quick rise to prominence in Darius's government made him a marked man among that king's other advisers. Daniel, however, proved himself adept at negotiating palace intrigue.

Some things, however, are nonnegotiable.

Daniel could not follow this royal edict: "Any person who prays to anyone but the king shall be thrown into the lions' den." The decree dreamed up by a faction of rogue advisers was nothing more than a shrewd political maneuver—a way for Daniel's enemies to create a fatal trap. But the king didn't know that when he put it into writing, making it an inviolable law. He didn't realize that his favorite adviser, Daniel, prayed three times a day to the God of Israel—in front of an open window that faced Jerusalem.

Daniel certainly recognized the decree for what it was. He knew his opponents had found a way to use his devotion to God against him. He understood that the next time he prayed could be his last. So he faced a choice: embrace his God-honoring practices and endure the consequences or hide his beliefs and play it safe.

For Daniel, there was no debating. As soon as the new law was announced, he went straight to his room, dropped to his knees, and prayed to the Lord—in full view of his enemies, who were watching him carefully.

The rest of the story is well documented. King Darius, much to his dismay, was forced to throw Daniel into a pit of hungry lions and then seal the pit with a stone. (It seems that a decree by the king could not be rescinded—not even by the king himself.) Darius returned to his palace and spent a sleepless night worrying about his trusted adviser. At the first light of dawn, he rushed back to the pit.

> When he reached the den, he cried out in anguish to Daniel. "Daniel, servant of the living God," the king said, "has your God whom you serve continually been able to rescue you from the lions?"
>
> Then Daniel spoke with the king: "May the king live forever. My God sent His angel and shut the lions' mouths. They haven't hurt me, for I was found innocent before Him. Also, I have not committed a crime against you my king." (Dan 6:20–22)

Daniel's willingness to die for his faith and God's willingness to save his faithful servant made a powerful impact on the king. His first order of business was to sentence to death—in the lions' den—the men who had brought the charges against Daniel, along with their families. His second order of business?

> Then King Darius wrote to those of every people, nation, and language who live in all the earth: "May your prosperity abound. I issue a decree that in all my royal dominion, people must tremble in fear before the God of Daniel:
>
> > For He is the living God,
> > and He endures forever;
> > His kingdom will never be destroyed,
> > and His dominion has no end.
> > He rescues and delivers;
> > He performs signs and wonders
> > in the heavens and on the earth,
> > for He has rescued Daniel
> > from the power of the lions." (Dan 6:25–27)

THE TAKEAWAY

Taking a bold stand for God *always* pays dividends. That's not to suggest that a miraculous outcome like Daniel's awaits everyone who stands firm in the face of overwhelming opposition. Millions of Christian martyrs could testify to that fact.

Yet one person's stand has the power to inspire others, to change hearts, and to produce results far beyond immediate circumstances. The better prepared you are to take a stand for your faith when circumstances dictate, the bigger the impact you can have.

FOOD FOR THOUGHT

1. What's the most dangerous or difficult situation you've ever faced as a believer? How did you respond?

2. What did you learn from the experience? What, if anything, would you do differently next time?

3. What steps can you take to prepare for the next difficult situation?

SHADRACH, MESHACH, AND ABEDNEGO

INTO THE FIRE

"If the God we serve exists, then He can rescue us from the furnace of blazing fire, and He can rescue us from the power of you, the king. But even if He does not rescue us, we want you as king to know that we will not serve your gods or worship the gold statue you set up." — Daniel 3:16–18

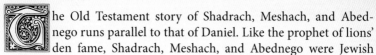

The Old Testament story of Shadrach, Meshach, and Abednego runs parallel to that of Daniel. Like the prophet of lions' den fame, Shadrach, Meshach, and Abednego were Jewish captives living in Babylon. Like Daniel, they earned positions as wise and trustworthy advisers of the king of Babylon. And like him, they inspired envy and enmity among their Babylonian counterparts in the king's government.

When Nebuchadnezzar commissioned a 90-foot-tall gold statue and ordered everyone in his kingdom to bow down and worship it, certain schemers in his government saw an opportunity to rid themselves of the three Israelites once and for all.

These nefarious advisers reported to the king that Shadrach, Meshach, and Abednego had refused to bow to his golden idol. They urged the king to sentence the three men to death in a blazing furnace, as was dictated by the king's decree.

Enraged, the king sent for Shadrach, Meshach, and Abednego and issued an ultimatum: "When you hear the sound of . . . every kind of music, fall down and worship the statue I made. But if you don't worship it, you will immediately be thrown into a furnace of blazing fire—and who is the god who can rescue you from my power?" (Dan 3:15).

Here's the reply he received: "Nebuchadnezzar, we don't need to give you an answer to this question. If the God we serve exists, then He can rescue us from the furnace of blazing fire, and He can rescue us from the power of you, the king" (Dan 3:16–17).

On the surface, those seem like brave words. Shadrach, Meshach, and Abednego courageously testified that God was powerful enough to save them from their imminent execution. But they likely saw nothing re-markable about their response. After all, they had historical precedence on their side.

From the time they were born, they'd heard about the God who had parted the Red Sea, sent a gushing stream of water from a rock in the desert, and fed his people with bread from heaven. Compared to those things, disabling a furnace probably seemed like a minor miracle.

The true essence of bold faith is found in what the three men said to the king next: "But even if He does not rescue us, we want you as king to know that we will not serve your gods or worship the gold statue you set up" (Dan 3:18).

"But even if He does not"—*there's* the heart of the matter. *There's* the essence of bold faith. It's one thing to approach a blazing furnace knowing you're going to be rescued in the nick of time. But Shadrach, Meshach, and Abednego had no such certainty. As far as they knew, they were about to die in a most excruciating way. Yet they remained faithful to God. Their devotion to him could not be shaken—not even by fear of death.

In the end, God delivered his three faithful servants in a way that left no doubt as to his power. Nebuchadnezzar gave orders to stoke the furnace seven times hotter than normal. The heat was so intense that the men who carried Shadrach, Meshach, and Abednego to the furnace's opening were killed instantly. Shadrach, Meshach, and Abednego, however, were able to walk around—unharmed—in the furnace. And they weren't alone.

When Nebuchadnezzar looked into the blaze, he saw a fourth man, one who looked "like a son of the gods" (Dan 3:25), walking with them. He called for Shadrach, Meshach, and Abednego to come out. When they did, he and all the other witnesses who had gathered to watch them burn saw that not a single hair on their heads or a thread on their clothes had been singed.

The effect of their bold decision can be seen in the astonished response of King Nebuchadnezzar:

> "Praise to the God of Shadrach, Meshach, and Abednego! He sent His angel and rescued His servants who trusted in Him. They violated the king's command and risked their lives rather than serve or worship any god except their own God. Therefore I issue a decree that anyone of any people, nation, or language who says anything offensive against the God of Shadrach, Meshach, and Abednego will be torn limb from limb and his house made a garbage dump. For there is no other god who is able to deliver like this." (Dan 3:28–29)

THE TAKEAWAY

Your relationship with the Lord will almost certainly cost you *something* at some point in your life. Depending on your circumstances, it may cost you the following (and more):

- A relationship

- Your popularity in certain circles

- Your comfort

- Your carefully laid plans

Yet God's promise to reward the faithful, whether in this life or the next, makes even the most extreme sacrifice pale in comparison.

FOOD FOR THOUGHT

1. What's the most extreme sacrifice you've ever seen anyone make for his or her Christian faith?

2. Why is sacrifice necessary?

3. What are you willing to sacrifice for your faith?

JONAH

RUNNING FROM GOD

"But as for me, I will sacrifice to You with a voice of thanksgiving. I will fulfill what I have vowed. Salvation is from the LORD!" — Jonah 2:9

onah stands alone among the prophets of the Old Testament. Certainly he was the only one (that we know of) to spend three days in the digestive tract of a fish. In the bigger picture, though, he was the only one (that we know of) to flatly refuse an assignment from God.

The Lord instructed Jonah to go to Nineveh to preach. Specifically, he told Jonah to preach against the people of Nineveh because their wickedness offended him. Instead, Jonah booked passage on a boat heading to Tarshish—that is, away from Nineveh. Some part of him must have believed—or at least desperately hoped—that he could escape his prophetic assignment.

The reason Jonah didn't want to go to Nineveh is as unexpected as it is perverse. It doesn't appear he was afraid for his safety or afraid of being rejected or humiliated. Quite the opposite, in fact.

The message God had given him was a dire warning to the people of Nineveh: *If you don't repent of your wicked ways, you will be destroyed.* And Jonah had a pretty good inkling of what would happen when the Ninevites heard the message. Their eyes would be opened. Their consciences would be touched. Their hearts would be moved. They would repent, exactly as God told them to do. Thus, they would receive his mercy, instead of his judgment.

In other words, the bad guys would be pardoned.

Nineveh was the capital city of Assyria, Israel's bitter enemy. The Assyrians had plagued the Israelites for centuries. The prospect of an entire Assyrian city being destroyed by God's judgment must have been tantalizing to a loyal son of Israel like Jonah. Likewise, the prospect of the entire city being spared by God because of something he (Jonah) did must have seemed absolutely intolerable to him.

That would explain why he ran.

He didn't get far. The boat to Tarshish encountered foul weather as soon as it hit the open sea. The boat's crewmen recognized that what they were facing was no ordinary storm. They sensed a divine judgment in the squall that threatened to sink their vessel. They cast lots (a common practice in those days) to determine which of their passengers was the focus of wrath. The results pointed to Jonah.

Jonah resigned himself to his fate. *Throw me overboard*, he advised the crew, *and the storm will cease.* The sailors resisted at first, but they finally had no choice. They threw Jonah over the side.

When Jonah plunged into the sea, two things happened: the waters immediately grew calm, and Jonah was swallowed by a giant fish. Jonah 1:17 says he spent three days inside the creature. That's a lot of time for a man to assess his life and rethink some of the choices he has made.

Jonah prayed to God from his rancid surroundings. He was through with running. If the Lord wanted him to go to Nineveh, that's where he would go—though it should be noted that his attitude toward the Ninevites seems to have remained unchanged. The fish vomited Jonah back on shore, and Jonah headed for Nineveh, where he watched his worst-case scenario unfold before his eyes.

Jonah delivered God's warning, according to his instructions. He walked through the city proclaiming God's judgment, which would come in 40 days unless the Ninevites repented.

The Ninevites rightly responded as if their lives depended on it. According to Jonah 3:5, "The men of Nineveh believed in God. They proclaimed a fast and dressed in sackcloth—from the greatest of them to the least." Fasting and wearing sackcloth demonstrated extreme humility and repentance.

The king of Nineveh removed his royal robes, wore sackcloth, and sat in the dust of the ground. He urged the people of Nineveh to call on God to withhold his judgment and to spare Nineveh.

Much to Jonah's displeasure, God honored their prayers. Jonah 3:10 says, "God relented from the disaster He had threatened to do to them. And He did not do it." The people of Nineveh lived to see another day, thanks to God's great forgiveness and mercy—and, to a much lesser degree, thanks to Jonah's effective proclamations.

THE TAKEAWAY

God's plan for your life will take you outside your comfort zone, perhaps frequently. God will put you in situations that force you to resist your natural instincts. He will ask you to do things you never expected. If you're not prepared to be unsettled, or to sacrifice your own desires for the greater good, you may struggle, as Jonah did. If you insist on clinging to your own agenda, you will miss out on the blessings God has in store for you.

If, on the other hand, you're willing to cede control to him, you'll find that God will work in and through you to accomplish some extraordinary things.

FOOD FOR THOUGHT

1. What's the most difficult thing you've ever felt called to do because of your Christian faith?

2. Describe a time when you tried to resist doing what you knew God wanted you to do. What did you learn from the experience?

3. What advice would you give to someone questioning God's calling?

JOSEPH (MARY'S HUSBAND)

OUT OF THE SPOTLIGHT

"*The birth of Jesus Christ came about this way: After His mother Mary had been engaged to Joseph, it was discovered before they came together that she was pregnant by the Holy Spirit. So her husband Joseph, being a righteous man, and not wanting to disgrace her publicly, decided to divorce her secretly.*

"*But after he had considered these things, an angel of the Lord suddenly appeared to him in a dream, saying, 'Joseph, son of David, don't be afraid to take Mary as your wife, because what has been conceived in her is by the Holy Spirit. She will give birth to a son, and you are to name Him Jesus, because He will save His people from their sins.'*" — *Matthew 1:18–21*

he circumstances of Jesus' birth seem to cast Joseph in a supporting role in God's plan. "Supporting," however, should not be confused with "inconsequential." Though Joseph's name doesn't appear often in the New Testament, the fact remains that God chose him for a reason. Jesus' heavenly Father selected Joseph to serve as Jesus' earthly parent. As such, Joseph played a pivotal role in Jesus' life.

He just did so away from the spotlight.

Mary wasn't the only one who received a visit from an angel prior to Jesus' birth. God sent a heavenly messenger to assure Joseph that Mary's pregnancy was not only legitimate but also a world-changing event. So Joseph stood with Mary, despite the inevitable gossip and attacks on his character that surely came with his decision. He risked his reputation and standing in the community for the sake of God's plan.

In the Christmas story, much is made of Jesus' humble birth in a place where animals were fed. What's not often mentioned is the fact that Joseph was canny enough to find a safe place for his expectant wife in Bethlehem, which had been overrun with crowds coming to register for taxation, as per Caesar Augustus's decree.

Joseph's plan was to return to Nazareth with Mary and the newborn Jesus after their brief stay in Bethlehem. However, he learned from an angel in a dream that Herod was intent on killing all baby boys to prevent the rise of the "King of the Jews" (Matt 2:2). Following the angel's instructions, Joseph immediately relocated his family to Egypt and stayed there until the threat ended. Joseph went to great lengths to protect the family that God had entrusted to him.

His fatherly concern can be seen clearly in the story of Jesus' boyhood visit to the temple in Jerusalem. Joseph and his family had traveled to Jerusalem in a caravan to celebrate Passover. On the journey home, Joseph and Mary couldn't find Jesus. So they returned to Jerusalem, where they eventually located him in the temple, astounding the Jewish religious leaders with his knowledge and understanding.

> His mother said to [Jesus], "Son, why have You treated us like this? Your father and I have been anxiously searching for You."

> "Why were you searching for Me?" He asked them. "Didn't you know that I had to be in My Father's house?" (Luke 2:48–49)

Joseph shared Mary's concern for Jesus' well-being, and likely her confusion and amazement at Jesus' precocious abilities.

It seems Joseph was a hands-on father to Jesus. The two likely spent hours together every day in Joseph's carpentry shop. Joseph almost certainly taught Jesus the skills he needed to make a living as a carpenter.

Joseph also gave Jesus an identity of sorts. When Jesus returned to Nazareth during his public ministry, the people there still remembered him—even if they were suspicious of his new spiritual authority. "Isn't this the carpenter's son?" (Matt 13:55), they asked one another. In their minds, Jesus' identity was still linked to Joseph's.

Bible scholars believe Joseph died before Jesus started his public ministry. If that is true, he didn't get a chance to see the fruition of what he helped nurture through the early days of Jesus' life.

Yet traces of Joseph's legacy can be seen. As Jesus hung on the cross, enduring unimaginable physical, emotional, and spiritual agony, he summoned the strength to make one last heartfelt request of his disciple John, who stood nearby.

As the eldest son of his earthly family, Jesus instructed John to take care of his mother, Mary, after his death. He concerned himself with the well-being of those in his care, just as his father, Joseph, had done three decades earlier.

THE TAKEAWAY

There is no such thing as an insignificant role in God's plan. Believers who use their spiritual gifts out of the public eye are just as essential as those in the spotlight. No act of mercy, no use of a spiritual gift, and no personal sacrifice ever goes unnoticed by God.

If you wonder about your significance in God's plan, ask the Lord to show you the difference you're making and the example you're setting for others.

FOOD FOR THOUGHT

1. First Corinthians 12 explains that Christians are all parts of Christ's body. If you were to take that concept literally, what body part would you say you are? Explain.

2. How does your role in Christ's body suit your personality?

3. What specific things can you do to encourage people whose work for the Lord often goes overlooked?

93

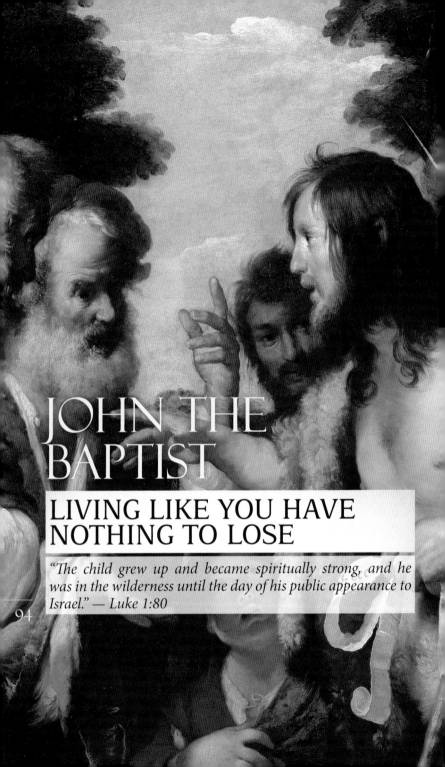

JOHN THE BAPTIST

LIVING LIKE YOU HAVE NOTHING TO LOSE

"The child grew up and became spiritually strong, and he was in the wilderness until the day of his public appearance to Israel." — Luke 1:80

he Gospel writer Luke precedes his account of Jesus' birth with that of a lesser (though still prominent) figure in Jewish prophecy: the forerunner who would prepare the way for the Messiah and announce his arrival.

The circumstances of this forerunner's birth were memorable. His mother, Elizabeth, was a relative of Jesus' mother, Mary. His father, Zechariah, served as a priest in the temple. One day the angel Gabriel appeared to Zechariah to announce that he and his wife would have a son. When Zechariah asked how that could be possible, since he and Elizabeth were well past the age when most people become parents, Gabriel told him he would be mute until his son was born because of his unbelief (see Luke 1:5–20).

Zechariah and Elizabeth named their son John. In time, he would become known as John the Baptist.

From a distance, John the Baptist may seem like an inscrutable New Testament eccentric—a cross between a slightly deranged street-corner preacher and a hardcore wilderness survivalist. The man lived in the desert outskirts of civilization. He wore a cloak made of camel's hair and a leather belt. He ate locusts and wild honey.

A closer look at John, however, reveals a person whose passion and struggles are quite relatable—and whose example deserves careful consideration. John understood from an early age that he was set apart by God for a purpose. It seems his whole life was geared to fulfilling that purpose.

Blessed with a sense of the Lord's plan of salvation for the world, John was among the first to know that the long-awaited Messiah had finally come (see John 1:29). For the Jewish people of the first century, there was no bigger news. By the same token, though, John also was one of the few people who understood that the Jewish people weren't ready for what was about to happen.

His God-given mandate was to ready the people of Israel—and he took the responsibility seriously. He challenged the people of Israel to turn away from their sin and publicly demonstrate their repentance by being baptized. Hundreds responded to his message.

One day Jesus showed up at John's ministry site near the Jordan River and asked John to baptize him. With genuine humility, John admitted that he was unworthy to baptize Jesus, who had nothing to repent of because he had never sinned. When Jesus explained that his baptism was part of God's plan, John fulfilled his responsibility (see Matt 3:13–17).

With the advent of Jesus' public ministry, John grew bolder in his own work. He challenged Herod, the king of Judea, to repent of his sins—specifically, his illegal marriage to the ex-wife of his brother.

John paid a steep price for his boldness. He was thrown into prison, where his body and spirit suffered tremendously. At his lowest point, he sent his disciples to Jesus to get assurance that Jesus was indeed the Messiah.

But that momentary display of weakness makes John's boldness throughout the rest of his life all the more remarkable. He understood that he'd been entrusted with the greatest news the world had ever received. He was not about to let concerns for his own safety, well-being, or likability get in the way of his responsibilities.

He refused to back down, even though he was angering the most powerful people in Israel. He spoke the words God had given him as powerfully and effectively as he could and left the consequences in God's hands.

Eventually John paid the ultimate price for his radical boldness and obedience. Herod was inclined to keep him alive, perhaps because he recognized the power and authority behind John's words. Herod's illegitimate wife had other ideas. She devised a scheme that involved her daughter dancing for Herod, something that pleased the king greatly.

When Herod promised to give the young dancer anything she requested, her mother instructed her to ask for the head of John the Baptist on a plate. His hand forced, Herod ordered the execution of the wilderness prophet.

Yet death could do little to diminish John's legacy. "I tell you, among those born of women no one is greater than John" (Luke 7:28). Those words came from Jesus himself, who understood better than anyone else how difficult it is to stand boldly in the face of opposition.

THE TAKEAWAY

Living your Christian faith with a spirit of boldness and courage can make a lasting impression on the people you encounter. If you unashamedly let your faith dictate the way you live, you may find that you inspire similar boldness in other believers—while also gaining the curiosity of unbelievers.

As John the Baptist demonstrated, when you represent God, you have no reason to be fearful or timid. Ultimately, no opposition can stand against you.

FOOD FOR THOUGHT

1. What happens when people take a timid or self-conscious approach to their Christian faith?

2. How can Christians who aren't bold by nature project a spirit of boldness in their faith?

3. What specific steps can you take to be bolder in your faith?

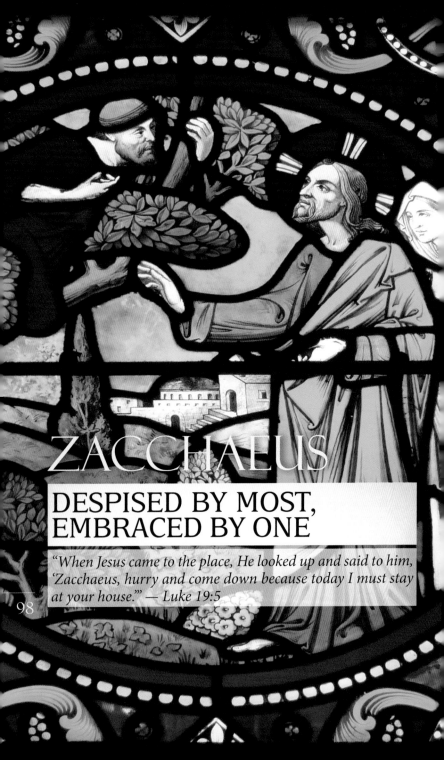

ZACCHAEUS

DESPISED BY MOST, EMBRACED BY ONE

"When Jesus came to the place, He looked up and said to him, 'Zacchaeus, hurry and come down because today I must stay at your house.'" — Luke 19:5

Zacchaeus was a chief tax collector, which means he likely was one of the least popular citizens of Jericho. Jewish people in the first century AD despised tax collectors. They not only did the work of the hated Roman Empire but also overcharged their fellow Jews and pocketed the extra money. That's why Luke describes Zacchaeus as "rich" (Luke 19:2). He likely built his wealth from the funds he stole from the people in his community.

When he heard that Jesus would be passing through his city, Zacchaeus had an overwhelming desire to see him. Unfortunately, his small stature made it difficult for him to peer over the crowds that had gathered for a glimpse of the Rabbi who had made such a name for himself throughout Israel.

So Zacchaeus climbed a sycamore tree, which not only gave him a chance to see Jesus but also gave Jesus a chance to see him. Imagine the emotions Zacchaeus experienced when the Lord looked up, called him by name, and told him he would be visiting his house that very day.

Murmurs ran through the crowd, many of whom likely had been victims of Zacchaeus's schemes and extortion. Why would Jesus choose to honor a despicable excuse for a human like Zacchaeus by staying at his house? Why would he befriend a sinful man when there were so many "good" people with whom he could spend time?

If anyone had been paying attention to Zacchaeus's response, he or she might have figured out the answer. The greedy, extorting tax collector was rocked to the core by Jesus' gracious gesture. He felt the full weight of the wrongs he'd committed and an overwhelming desire to repent and make things right.

Zacchaeus welcomed Jesus to his home right away. Then he pledged to give one-half of everything he owned to the poor and to repay the people he'd cheated four times the amount he took.

In Zacchaeus's reaction, we see the truth of Jesus' words in Mark 2:17: "Those who are well don't need a doctor, but the sick do need one. I didn't come to call the righteous, but sinners." Zacchaeus received salvation that day. Jesus said, "Today salvation has come to this house. . . . For the Son of Man has come to seek and to save the lost" (Luke 19:9–10).

The Bible doesn't specifically mention Zacchaeus again, but we can be certain that Zacchaeus made good on his promise to repay those he cheated and give generously to those in need.

THE TAKEAWAY

Though Jesus' entire interaction with Zacchaeus spans only 10 verses in the Bible, the encounter yields a wealth of applicable principles. Here are three.

1. When you sincerely seek the Lord, he will find you.

Something more than casual curiosity propelled Zacchaeus up that tree. Perhaps he'd heard of the changed lives that had been left in Jesus' wake. Perhaps he sensed the need for a change in his own life. Perhaps he dared to imagine that his lifetime of greed and selfishness could be redeemed.

Something compelled him to make sure he saw Jesus—and that Jesus saw him. Jesus didn't disappoint. He recognized Zacchaeus's deepest needs—for repentance and restoration—and laid the groundwork for those needs to be met.

2. There is no "us and them" where Jesus is concerned.

In first-century Jewish society, Zacchaeus was an undesirable, an outcast, someone "good" people were supposed to shun. Those who violated the rules of polite society and dared to interact with outcasts ran the risk of becoming outcasts themselves.

So Jesus' interaction with Zacchaeus must have been both startling and eye-opening to his followers. He singled out arguably the most despicable man in the crowd for a personal visit. He sought the company of someone most people avoided.

Jesus didn't just violate the rules of polite society by rubbing shoulders with undesirables; he refused even to acknowledge them as undesirables. He flattened the hierarchy of Jewish society. He erased the lines that people drew to separate themselves from others and make themselves look superior. And he set an example for all who follow him.

3. A sincere heart is the key to transformation.

Jesus didn't tell Zacchaeus what to do. The idea of giving half of his possessions to the poor and paying back four times the amount he extorted from people came from Zacchaeus himself. Zacchaeus saw an opportunity to change his life, and he was willing to sacrifice everything he owned to make it happen.

Jesus honored his sincere desire for forgiveness and salvation. He offered Zacchaeus a fresh start and a clean slate, and he will do the same for anyone who comes to him with a sincere desire to change.

FOOD FOR THOUGHT

1. Who are the outcasts in your community—the people who are ignored or shunned by polite society?

2. If Jesus lived in your community, how do you think he would interact with those people? Be as specific as possible. What do you imagine him doing for them? What do you imagine him saying to them?

3. What specific steps can you take to represent Jesus to the outcasts in your community?

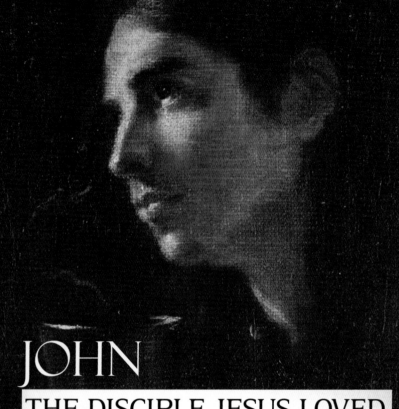

JOHN
THE DISCIPLE JESUS LOVED

"But Peter and John answered them, 'Whether it's right in the sight of God for us to listen to you rather than to God, you decide; for we are unable to stop speaking about what we have seen and heard.'" — Acts 4:19–20

ohn wasn't always known as "the disciple Jesus loved." Jesus called him and his brother the "Sons of Thunder" (Mark 3:17), likely because of their fiery tempers. Fits of temper occasionally landed John in trouble, such as the time he wanted to call down a fiery judgment from heaven on a Samaritan village that refused to welcome Jesus (see Luke 9:51–56).

John, a blue-collar worker like most of the other disciples, was a fisherman from Capernaum. He recognized the rare privileges he enjoyed as part of Jesus' inner circle. John was present for Jesus' transfiguration. He heard the voice of God. He saw the heavenly Father's glory physically manifested in Jesus.

Perhaps due to the elite company he kept, John occasionally struggled to keep his ego in check. He once tried to stop a man from doing the Lord's work simply because the man wasn't an official disciple. He and his brother James earned the ire of the other disciples when their mother requested exclusive places of honor for them in Jesus' future kingdom.

But those incidents merely reflected the spiritual growing pains of a man coming to grips with the extraordinary opportunities and responsibilities that were laid out before him.

Through it all, John maintained a fierce loyalty and unshakable closeness to Jesus. It should come as no surprise, then, that he emerged as a go-to guy among the disciples. When the time came to prepare the Passover feast that became the Last Supper, Jesus put John in charge of making the arrangements. More significantly, while Jesus hung on the cross, he entrusted John with the responsibility of taking care of his mother, Mary, after his death.

When the news of Jesus' resurrection reached the disciples, John was the first one to reach the empty tomb (see John 20:1–5). Perhaps he sensed that the end of Jesus' earthly ministry would be the start of his own.

After Jesus ascended to heaven, John emerged as one of the leaders of first-century Christianity. The book of Acts records his early ministry efforts with his fellow disciple Peter. In the Lord's name, they healed a lame man at the temple in Jerusalem. Everywhere they went, they spoke to crowds about Jesus and salvation through him—at considerable risk to themselves.

The persecution of Christians was underway. Those who identified themselves with the fledgling Christian movement were subject to imprisonment, torture, and death.

When John was arrested and stood before the Sanhedrin to defend his actions, he acquitted himself masterfully (as did Peter). According to Acts 4:13, "When they observed the boldness of Peter and John and realized that they were uneducated and untrained men, they were amazed and recognized that they had been with Jesus."

The apostle Paul cited John as one of the "pillars" of the Christian church (Gal 2:9). In time, John became an elder statesman of sorts—a trusted adviser to various first-century evangelists and congregations.

John was tapped to write one of the four definitive accounts of Jesus' life. It is through his words that many people come to know Christ. In addition to the Gospel of John, three New Testament epistles—1 John, 2 John, and 3 John—as well as the apocalyptic book of Revelation are credited to the faithful fisherman from Capernaum.

Church history tells us that John was the only apostle who did not die a martyr's death. Instead, he was banished to the prison island of Patmos, where he lived out his final days—faithful to the end.

THE TAKEAWAY

John proved himself utterly reliable in his daily interaction with Jesus. He was rough around the edges, as were all of Jesus' disciples. He faced the occasional rebuke from Jesus. But he learned from his mistakes. He grew in his faith. He made himself a valuable member of Jesus' ministry team, as well as a trusted confidante of the Lord himself.

In the spirit of Matthew 25:23—"Well done, good and faithful slave! You were faithful over a few things; I will put you in charge of many things. Share your master's joy!"—John's responsibilities increased with his spiritual growth.

The same principle applies today. If you prove yourself faithful to the Lord in your daily decisions, interactions with others, commitments to prayer and Bible study, and efforts to use your spiritual gifts and abilities, you will experience exponential growth in your relationship with him. What's more, you will be given a more substantial role in his work.

FOOD FOR THOUGHT

1. Give some examples of daily decisions and interactions that offer you opportunities to demonstrate your faithfulness to Jesus.

2. What might a "more substantial role in Jesus' work" involve? How would you feel about taking on such responsibilities?

3. Explain what it would mean to you to hear Jesus say, "Well done, good and faithful slave! You were faithful over a few things; I will put you in charge of many things. Share your master's joy!"

THOMAS

BELIEF INTERRUPTED

"One of the Twelve, Thomas (called 'Twin'), was not with them when Jesus came. So the other disciples kept telling him, 'We have seen the Lord!'

"But he said to them, 'If I don't see the mark of the nails in His hands, put my finger into the mark of the nails, and put my hand into His side, I will never believe!'" — John 20:24–25

For all we know, Thomas may have been the boldest of Jesus' 12 disciples—a paragon of courageous service and unshakable loyalty. The New Testament offers evidence to support the notion. After Jesus raised Lazarus from the dead, some of the disciples were reluctant to return to Judea, where an attempt had been made on Jesus' life. Thomas was the one who finally said, "Let's go so that we may die with Him" (John 11:16).

It could be that Thomas was the best listener of Jesus' disciples. After Jesus told his followers that he was returning to heaven to prepare a place for them and that they knew the way to where he was going, Thomas was the one who spoke up: "Lord . . . we don't know where You're going. How can we know the way?" (John 14:5). Maybe the same question occurred to the other disciples; maybe it didn't. Either way, only Thomas showed he was paying attention.

The full scope of Thomas's contributions and strengths as a disciple will forever be overshadowed by one moment of weakness. Thomas is remembered first and foremost as Jesus' doubting disciple.

Thomas was absent the first time Jesus appeared to his disciples after his resurrection. When the others tried to tell Thomas about their post-resurrection encounter with the Lord, he was (perhaps understandably) reluctant to believe their story. In fact, he adamantly rejected their eye-witness accounts. He said, "If I don't see the mark of the nails in His hands, put my finger into the mark of the nails, and put my hand into His side, I will never believe!" (John 20:25).

File that statement under *Be Careful What You Ask For*.

Eight days later, the disciples assembled again. This time Thomas was with them. Jesus appeared once more and presented himself to Thomas for inspection. Jesus said, "Put your finger here and observe My hands. Reach out your hand and put it into My side. Don't be an unbeliever, but a believer" (John 20:27).

Imagine Thomas's elation as he heard his vow of skepticism and doubt referenced in the words of the risen Lord. The chastised disciple's disbelief vanished forever. "Thomas responded to Him, 'My Lord and my God!'" (John 20:28).

Even that wonderfully sincere statement of faith was not enough to change history's view of him. So he is forever known not as "Faithful Thomas" or even "Astonished Thomas" but as "Doubting Thomas."

Perhaps even more touching than Thomas's change of heart is Jesus' reaction to his doubt. He didn't punish Thomas for his staunch refusal to believe. He didn't revoke Thomas's disciple card. He didn't verbally berate Thomas for his temporary doubt.

Instead, he equipped Thomas with the evidence he needed to believe. In effect, Jesus said, *If examining the nail wounds in my hands will make you feel more secure in your faith, then look as closely as you like at them. And if touching the spot where the spear pierced my side will convince you that I have done what I promised to do, then touch it. I have a vital role for you in my ministry, Thomas, and I will give you what you need to carry out that ministry.*

Church history tells us that Thomas did indeed play a key role in the spread of Christianity in the first century AD. According to tradition, he carried the good news of Jesus to Persia (and perhaps even as far as India), where he was eventually executed for his missionary work. In the end, not even the threat of death could shake Thomas's renewed faith in the risen Christ.

THE TAKEAWAY

Doubt isn't necessarily the opposite of faith. Sometimes it's a quick pit stop on the way to a deeper faith. No matter where you are on the assuredness spectrum, at some point in your life you will likely face circumstances that shake your belief or cause you to question God.

The good news is that God understands your doubts. The better news is that he can and will help you work through those doubts. Take your concerns and questions to him in prayer. Ask him to help you. You may find that you emerge from your season of doubt with a stronger faith in the Lord—and a deeper empathy for others who struggle.

FOOD FOR THOUGHT

1. Describe the last time you experienced a season of doubt. What were the circumstances that brought on the doubt? What questions or concerns created an obstacle in your relationship with the Lord?

2. What did you learn from the experience? What would you do differently the next time you experience a season of doubt?

3. What specific advice would you give to someone who admits to struggling to hold on to faith in the risen Christ?

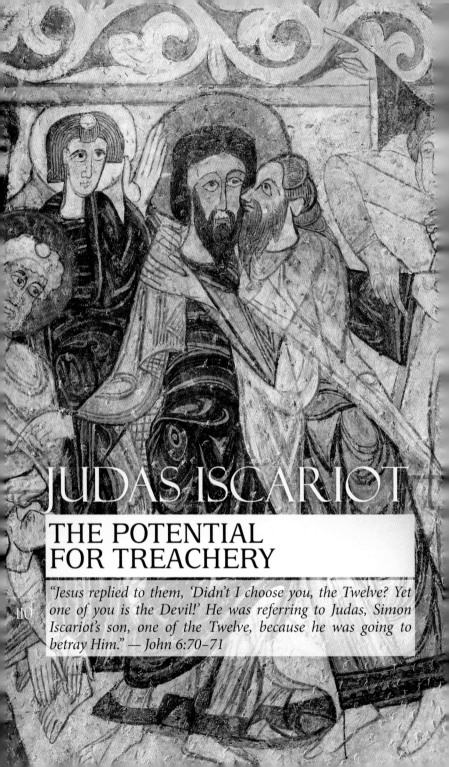

JUDAS ISCARIOT

THE POTENTIAL
FOR TREACHERY

"Jesus replied to them, 'Didn't I choose you, the Twelve? Yet one of you is the Devil!' He was referring to Judas, Simon Iscariot's son, one of the Twelve, because he was going to betray Him." — John 6:70–71

he story of Judas Iscariot may be the most unsettling cautionary tale in all of Scripture. For three years, Judas spent practically every day in the presence of the Son of God—experiencing his miracles, listening to his teachings, and watching him change lives and give hope to multitudes.

Yet even with such enviable access and spiritual training, Judas proved himself capable of committing perhaps the most heinous act of betrayal in human history. He secured his place in the pantheon of villainy by turning Jesus over to his enemies for 30 pieces of silver.

With that one act, he forever made his name synonymous with treachery and betrayal. Some two thousand years after the man's death, it's still considered a vile insult to be called a "Judas."

The origin of the name Iscariot, on the other hand, is a subject of debate among Bible scholars. Some believe it comes from *Kerioth*, which may have been a region in Judea. Others believe it identifies Judas with the *sicarii*, a group of assassins who wanted to drive the Romans from their Jewish homeland.

In addition to his betrayal of Jesus, Judas Iscariot plays a prominent role in another Gospel story, one found in John 12:1–8. Jesus and his disciples were dining in Bethany. Mary, the sister of Martha and Lazarus, carried in a jar of nard, an expensive perfume. She used the perfume to anoint Jesus' feet and then used her hair to wipe off the excess oil.

Hers was an extraordinary act of generosity and service, yet Judas could only see it as a foolish waste of money and asked, "Why wasn't this fragrant oil sold for 300 denarii and given to the poor?" (John 12:5).

Lest any of his readers mistake Judas's reaction for actual concern for the needy, the Gospel writer John (who knew Judas Iscariot very well) hastened to add, "He didn't say this because he cared about the poor but because he was a thief. He was in charge of the money-bag and would steal part of what was put in it" (John 12:6).

If Judas had been simply a petty thief or an embezzler of ministry funds, his historic profile would probably be much lower. But bad choices tend to have a snowball effect. They build on one another until they become impossible to control.

That may explain why Judas Iscariot conspired with Jesus' enemies to betray him. Judas agreed to lead a group into the garden of Gethsemane, where Jesus prayed, so they could arrest him. Within hours of his arrest, Jesus was put on trial, tortured by Roman soldiers, and nailed to a cross.

Bible scholars have long debated the reason for Judas Iscariot's actions. One of the few clues Scripture offers is found in Luke 22:3: "Then Satan entered Judas, called Iscariot, who was numbered among the Twelve." Beyond that, little is known about the thought process that went into Judas's plan.

What is known is that Jesus recognized Judas's traitorous nature early on. Look at John 6:70–71: "Jesus replied to them, 'Didn't I choose you, the Twelve? Yet one of you is the Devil!' He was referring to Judas, Simon Iscariot's son, one of the Twelve, because he was going to betray Him." As to why Jesus allowed Judas to be a part of his ministry in the first place, the Bible is silent.

Whatever Judas Iscariot's reason was for betraying Jesus, he felt nothing but shame and regret for his actions when they were completed. He tried to return the money he'd been given, but his coconspirators wouldn't take it back.

With no hope and no chance for redemption that he could see, Judas made one final terrible decision. According to Matthew 27:5, he "hanged himself."

THE TAKEAWAY

No matter how close you believe you are to Jesus, you must zealously guard against making destructive decisions and allowing momentary lapses of judgment. One bad decision tends to lead to increasingly worse decisions. Moral shortcuts that seem harmless at first almost always turn out to be anything but. Before you realize what's happening, you may find yourself in circumstances that are difficult or even impossible to undo.

The best way to avoid such circumstances is to carefully weigh your decisions, big and small, against what you know of Jesus. Spend quality time in his Word every day. Let its principles guide your decision making. Pray when you're tempted. Ask God for his strength to resist.

Likewise, the best way to deal with destructive decisions you've made in the past is to turn them over to the Lord. Seek forgiveness from those wronged by your actions. Ask God to help you turn away from your old habits and pursue a path that pleases him. Surround yourself with accountability partners to help you maintain focus.

FOOD FOR THOUGHT

1. What temptations or circumstances pose the biggest challenge to your Christian walk?

2. How have they gotten the upper hand in the past?

3. What specific steps can you take to prevent them from doing so in the future?

SIMON PETER

ORDINARY GUY, EXTRAORDINARY OPPORTUNITY

"And I also say to you that you are Peter, and on this rock I will build My church, and the forces of Hades will not overpower it." — Matthew 16:18

According to Matthew 4:18–20, "As [Jesus] was walking along the Sea of Galilee, He saw two brothers, Simon, who was called Peter, and his brother Andrew. They were casting a net into the sea, since they were fishermen. 'Follow Me,' He told them, 'and I will make you fish for people!' Immediately they left their nets and followed Him."

The fact that Jesus directed those words to a fisherman like Simon Peter—a rough-hewn, blue-collar type with no formal religious training and no elite position in Jewish society—says a lot about Jesus. He was not the type to surround himself with arrogant, status-obsessed priests and "experts" of Old Testament law like those to whom the Jews looked for religious guidance. He chose to change the world through a different type of person.

Jesus' call to discipleship also says something about Simon Peter. Jesus saw something in him that no one else—not even Peter himself—could see. Jesus saw Peter's potential. He looked past his exterior, his penchant for making rash decisions and folding under pressure, and into Peter's heart. There he saw abilities and a spirit of willingness that were valuable to him. He focused on qualities he could work with, abilities he could mold.

That first seaside encounter is perhaps the only unremarkable reference to Simon Peter in the Gospels. For better or worse, the man's personality leaps off the page of practically every Bible story that mentions him.

Simon Peter was a complex man. He proved himself to be courageous and loyal, yet capable of stunning lapses in judgment. His mercurial nature resulted in more than a few ups and downs in his relationship with Jesus. Yet if Simon Peter seems to be on the receiving end of more than his share of divine rebukes, it may be due to the fact that he dared to risk more than his fellow disciples.

Along with James and John, Simon Peter was part of Jesus' inner circle—the companions to whom he turned for support at critical times. Even among that trio, Simon Peter stood out. He may have been Jesus' best friend.

The New Testament contains more information about Peter than about the other 11 disciples *combined*. According to Matthew 8:14 and 1 Corinthians 9:5, for instance, Peter had a Christian wife who assisted him in his later missionary work. The Gospels mention nothing specific about the marital status of any other apostle.

In stories involving the disciples, Simon Peter is often at the center of the action. During the precarious crossing of the Sea of Galilee described in Matthew 14:22–32, only Simon Peter had the courage and desire to step out of the boat in the middle of a raging storm in order to walk on the water to Jesus.

When thoughts and questions occurred to him, Simon Peter didn't spend a lot of time in deep contemplation over them. He simply blurted them out. Sometimes that earned him high praise from the Lord, as when he declared Jesus to be "the Messiah, the Son of the living God" in Matthew 16:16. Other times it put him in the proverbial doghouse, such as when he dared to object to Jesus' prophecy of his impending death. Jesus' sharp rebuke, "Get behind Me, Satan!" (Matt 16:23), likely affected him deeply.

Aside from Judas Iscariot, probably no other apostle experienced the kind of despair and self-loathing that Simon Peter did after he denied knowing Jesus three times on the night the Lord was arrested and put on trial.

Yet Simon Peter didn't stay down for long. After Jesus' resurrection, he seized an opportunity to make amends with Jesus and restore their relationship. From that point on, the man was virtually unstoppable as a driving force in the first-century Christian movement. He fulfilled the destiny Jesus laid out for him in Matthew 16:18: "I also say to you that you are Peter, and on this rock I will build My church, and the forces of Hades will not overpower it."

Simon Peter boldly proclaimed Jesus' message throughout the Jewish world—and later throughout the Gentile world—until his own death. According to church tradition, Simon Peter was crucified upside down because he didn't believe he was worthy to be crucified in the same manner as his Lord.

THE TAKEAWAY

Simon Peter serves as a mirror for Christians who read the Gospels and the book of Acts. His decisions are relatable. His human nature is all too recognizable. His boldness and his cowardice touch our hearts.

In Peter, Christians can see their potential. For all his bluster, confusion, wrongheadedness, and mistakes, the man was deemed useful—even essential—by the Son of God. Jesus looked past his dross and saw the gold, just as he does for anyone who follows him. If you ever feel unworthy in your walk with Christ, look to the apostle Peter for inspiration.

FOOD FOR THOUGHT

1. What useful qualities might Jesus see in you? What could he accomplish using those qualities?

2. What mistakes or bad decisions have negatively affected your relationship with Jesus?

3. What comfort and encouragement can you draw from Simon Peter's experience?

PAUL

THE UNLIKELIEST DISCIPLE

"I have fought the good fight, I have finished the race, I have kept the faith. There is reserved for me in the future the crown of righteousness, which the Lord, the righteous Judge, will give me on that day, and not only to me, but to all those who have loved His appearing." — 2 Timothy 4:7–8

aul (or Saul, as he was also known) was a zealot, a staunch defender of the Jewish faith. He was especially zealous about exposing and punishing offshoots of Judaism that threatened to obscure its message.

He targeted the disciples of a rabbi named Jesus of Nazareth who were attempting to keep his message alive even after the rabbi himself had been crucified. They spread stories about seeing him risen from the dead. They claimed he was the Son of God and the way to everlasting life.

Saul was determined to stamp out the movement. He led the charge in persecuting "Christians," as they were later called (see Acts 11:26). He participated in the first recorded martyrdom in church history, the stoning of Stephen.

One day Paul set out for Damascus to arrest Christians and take them back to Jerusalem for punishment. His plans were derailed by a bright light from heaven that knocked him to the ground and left him temporarily blind.

> He heard a voice saying to him, "Saul, Saul, why are you persecuting Me?"
>
> "Who are You, Lord?" he said.
>
> "I am Jesus, the One you are persecuting," He replied. "But get up and go into the city, and you will be told what you must do." (Acts 9:4–6)

In Damascus, Saul was met by a believer named Ananias, who "placed his hands on him and said, 'Brother Saul, the Lord Jesus, who appeared to you on the road you were traveling, has sent me so that you can regain your sight and be filled with the Holy Spirit.' At once something like scales fell from his eyes, and he regained his sight. Then he got up and was baptized" (Acts 9:17–18).

Shortly thereafter, Paul started preaching about Jesus in the local synagogues. He didn't need much prep time. As a devoutly religious Jew, he knew the Scriptures. So once he recognized Jesus as the long-awaited Messiah, he was ready to share the good news.

People—including the apostles—were understandably skeptical at first. It didn't take long, though, for most to recognize that his transformation was real.

Thus began a life on the move, as Paul carried the gospel throughout Asia Minor and Europe. The book of Acts records three separate missionary journeys taken by Paul. On his first journey, a group of Jews who didn't like his message stoned him and dragged his body outside the city, thinking him dead. He wasn't—not by a long shot.

His original plan had been to preach the gospel in local synagogues, but the Jewish audiences rejected his message. Undeterred, he turned his attention to Gentile audiences, a decision that sent shock waves throughout the Christian world.

On his second journey, he and his fellow missionary Silas were beaten and imprisoned in Philippi. When an earthquake opened the doors of their cells and freed them from their chains, the two missionaries refused to escape. Their jailer was so moved by their gesture that he converted to Christianity on the spot.

Paul's third journey was marked by stunning miracles, including the healing of a young man who was thought to be dead. Paul experienced several near misses, including becoming a victim of a riot in Ephesus. The journey ended in Jerusalem, where Paul was beaten by a Jewish mob and arrested by Roman soldiers.

The biblical narrative ends before Paul stood trial. Church tradition suggests that he spent years as a prisoner in Rome before finally being executed during the reign of Nero around AD 67.

The apostle Paul founded or shepherded several different churches during his lifetime. When his journeys took him to a new destination, he maintained contact with congregations through letters. In those letters, Paul encouraged, taught, chastised, and challenged church members. At least 13 of Paul's letters are part of the New Testament canon.

From a logical perspective, Paul's experiences as an enemy of believers should have disqualified him from Christian service. God, however, saw his potential and not his past. And the rest is Christian history.

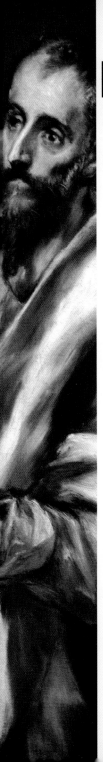

THE TAKEAWAY

No sin is too despicable for God to forgive. No reputation is too damaged to disqualify you from God's service. Paul was an accomplice to murder—a participant in the first recorded Christian martyrdom. He actively pursued and persecuted God's people and did his best to stamp out Christianity before it could gain a foothold.

Yet God chose him to spearhead the spread of Christianity throughout the world. The Lord worked in and through Paul to nurture the development of the church and to spell out the principles of Christian living.

Likewise, God can and will use you to accomplish extraordinary things in his name and for his kingdom—regardless of your past mistakes or your personal limitations—if you make yourself available to him.

FOOD FOR THOUGHT

1. How could you encourage someone who doubts their usefulness to God because of things in the past?

2. To what Scripture passages would you point them?

3. What experiences from your own life would you share to offer them reassurance?

JOHN MARK

THE COMEBACK KID

"Bring Mark with you, for he is useful to me in the ministry."
— *2 Timothy 4:11*

he Gospel of Mark describes a curious incident that took place on the night of Jesus' arrest in the garden of Gethsemane. As the mob of Jewish religious leaders and Roman soldiers started to drag Jesus away, they noticed a young man sneaking around in a linen garment. "They caught hold of him, but he left the linen cloth behind and ran away naked" (Mark 14:51–52).

The fact that the encounter is mentioned nowhere else in Scripture suggests that the young man who fled Gethsemane in shame (and very little else) may well have been the writer of the Gospel himself: John Mark.

As humiliating as that experience may have been, John Mark's story actually goes *downhill* from there. His family was well known in first-century Christian circles. When the apostle Peter was released from prison, he went to the house of John Mark's mother, Mary, because he knew he would find fellow believers there. John Mark (better known as Mark) likely rubbed shoulders with a number of Jesus' disciples and close friends.

He was also the younger cousin of Barnabas, a traveling companion of the apostle Paul and one of the leading evangelists of the day. As for Mark himself, little is known about his ministry experiences. It's difficult to say, then, whether it was nepotism or a legitimate reputation that got him invited to accompany Paul and Barnabas on their first missionary journey.

Acts 13:5 describes Mark as an "assistant." He may have served as a business manager or a scribe who recorded the words and deeds of Paul and Barnabas. Whatever he did, though, he didn't do it for long. When the team reached the city of Perga, Mark had a change of heart and returned to Jerusalem (see Acts 13:13).

Details about the split are scarce. The only clues the Bible offers are found in Acts 15:37–39. As Paul and Barnabas prepared for their second missionary journey together, Barnabas wanted to invite Mark to accompany them again; Paul vehemently opposed the idea. As far as he was concerned, Mark had deserted them on their previous journey and Paul didn't want it to happen again.

Neither Paul nor Barnabas would budge, and their disagreement turned sharp—so sharp, in fact, that the two decided to part ways. Paul teamed with Silas for his next journey, and Barnabas traveled to Cyprus with Mark.

And that's where Mark fades from the Bible's story line. The second half of the book of Acts follows Paul and his exploits. Mark isn't mentioned again.

As his ship set sail for Cyprus (see Acts 15:39), it seemed Mark's story was written. His legacy was sealed.

Except it wasn't.

Again, details are scarce. But what we do know is that at the end of his life, the apostle Paul was imprisoned in Rome. In his final letter to his dear friend Timothy, he poured out his feelings of loneliness and abandonment: "Make every effort to come to me soon, for Demas has deserted me, because he loved this present world, and has gone to Thessalonica. Crescens has gone to Galatia, Titus to Dalmatia. Only Luke is with me. Bring Mark with you, for he is useful to me in the ministry" (2 Tim 4:9–11).

Mark is useful to me.

In the years since their falling out, Mark had become a valuable ally to Paul. He had become someone who brought Paul joy and comfort. He had become a confidante, a friend, a peer.

That's the final verdict on Mark in Scripture.

After an unbelievably rough start, Mark orchestrated a comeback for the ages. Imagine how hard he worked to regain Paul's trust, to prove himself faithful, to change people's minds, and to forge a new legacy for himself.

God rewarded his diligence by giving him a key role in the burgeoning Christian movement. He tapped Mark to write one of the four official biographical accounts of Jesus. Drawing on the experiences of his old friend Peter, Mark crafted a Gospel that has introduced billions of people to God's Son. Mark's impact on Christianity is still being felt two thousand years later.

THE TAKEAWAY

John Mark's story demonstrates that no one is ever too far gone to stage a comeback. No mistake is too big to disqualify you from God's service. No sin is beyond God's willingness to forgive.

In fact, many people who have experienced a turnaround like Mark's find that their past failures have uniquely equipped them for service and ministry. No one can testify more convincingly about God's grace than someone who has experienced it.

That's a message people need to hear—and one of which believers need to remind themselves on a regular basis.

FOOD FOR THOUGHT

1. What practical advice would you give to someone who's struggling to overcome a personal failure?

2. Which aspects of Mark's story hit closest to home? Explain.

3. What have your failures taught you about God's grace?

JESUS

THE PERFECT EXAMPLE

"For we do not have a high priest who is unable to sympathize with our weaknesses, but One who has been tested in every way as we are, yet without sin." — Hebrews 4:15

esus was fully God when he came to earth. He was also fully human. He can empathize with our weaknesses and our limitations.

By the same token, he is also acutely aware of our potential as humans because he maximized his. He knows not just who we are and what we're like but also what we can become.

Jesus' teachings, scattered throughout the Gospels, offer an ideal blueprint for experiencing the absolute best God has to offer in this world. Jesus' *actions* offer even more. He demonstrated the truth of his words in the way he lived. He gave us a model to follow.

Here are four things Jesus did that can and should serve as an inspiration to his followers.

1. Jesus leaned heavily on God and his Word.

Jesus maintained open communication with his heavenly Father. His prayer times were essential to him. New Testament passages such as Mark 1:35 describe how he would get up before sunrise and steal away to a secluded location in order to spend quality time with God.

Just before his arrest, Jesus retreated to the garden of Gethsemane to pray for the strength to endure the agony and suffering that lay ahead. As he hung on the cross, suspended between life and death, he asked God to forgive his tormentors. Prayer was never far from the Lord's lips.

Jesus also made God's Word central to his life. As a young boy, he astounded the teachers of the law in the Jerusalem temple with his knowledge of Scripture. But he didn't just memorize God's Word; he used it. When Satan tempted him in the wilderness, Jesus quoted Old Testament passages to rebuff him and drive him away.

2. Jesus surrounded himself with people who shared his priorities.

He certainly didn't choose his disciples based on their experience, their standing in the community, or their likable personalities. He chose them based on their desire to see God's kingdom advanced in the world.

Granted, the men he chose may not have recognized that quality in themselves when Jesus called them, but Jesus could see it. He could sense their zeal, their faithfulness, their willingness to sacrifice their personal interests for the sake of Jesus' ministry. The camaraderie and friendships that blossomed among Jesus and his disciples over time sprang from their shared priorities.

3. Jesus focused on potential, not reputation.

The religious leaders of Jesus' day were appalled by the company he kept. He spent time with lepers, prostitutes, adulterers, the demon-possessed, Samaritans, tax collectors, and countless other people who were ignored or actively shunned by the "decent" religious folks of the day.

Jesus cared less about people's past mistakes or current status than about what they could become. His aim was not to punish people for their old life but to show them new life.

4. Jesus understood the power of sacrifice.

Jesus' death on the cross paid the price of sin for the entire world and makes salvation and eternal life possible. Yet before he gave his life to save others, Jesus demonstrated sacrificial love in countless ways.

He sacrificed his time and energy to make other people's lives better. Almost everywhere he went, Jesus was swarmed by people who wanted something from him, whether it was healing, forgiveness, spiritual truth, or just a moment of personal attention. Day after day Jesus attended to the needs of the masses.

His disciples saw firsthand the toll that the constant demands took on Jesus. Occasionally they tried to turn people away from him in order to let him rest. But Jesus insisted on being accessible to those who needed him.

Jesus sacrificed his standing in the community to embrace outcasts. He gave up his place in elite society—the "popular" crowd—by focusing his attention on the poor, the needy, the despised, and the overlooked.

John 15:13 says, "No one has greater love than this, that someone would lay down his life for his friends." Jesus understood better than anyone that nothing speaks love more loudly to people than sacrifice.

THE TAKEAWAY

The wisest course of action in any situation is to ask yourself, "What would Jesus do?" and then do everything in your power to emulate him. In order to do that, though, you must *know* Jesus. Take every opportunity to study the way he interacted with people, the way he spent his time, the things he said, and the things he *didn't* say. Spend time in his Word and in his presence through Bible study, prayer, and quiet times.

FOOD FOR THOUGHT

1. When it comes to following the example Jesus set, in which of the four areas are you strongest?

2. In which area(s) do you struggle most? What obstacles and challenges get in your way?

3. List one specific step you can take in each of the four areas to better emulate Jesus.

TOPICAL INDEX

132

SCRIPTURE INDEX

ART CREDITS

page 5
Meunierd / Shutterstock.com

page 6
jorisvo / Shutterstock.com

page 21
jorisvo / Shutterstock.com

page 29
Renata Sedmakova / Shutterstock.com

page 45
Zvonimir Atletic / Shutterstock.com

page 46
Saul Peter Horree / Alamy.com

page 48
Peter de Kievith / Istockphoto

page 55
Lebrecht Music and Arts Photo Library / Alamy.com

page 62
Renata Sedmakova / Shutterstock.com

page 64
audioscience / Shutterstock.com

page 80
Liszt collection / Alamy.com

page 90
Renata Sedmakova / Shutterstock.com

page 93
Renata Sedmakova / Shutterstock.com

page 100
Mary Evans Picture Library / Alamy.com

page 120
Peter Horree / Alamy.com

NOTES

NOTES

NOTES